Along
Country Lines

A DAVID & CHARLES BOOK

David & Charles is a subsidiary of F+W (UK) Ltd.,
an F+W Publications Inc. company

First published in the UK in 2005

Distributed in North America
by F+W Publications, Inc.
4700 East Galbraith Road
Cincinnati, OH 45236
1-800-289-0963

A catalogue record for this book is available from the
British Library.

ISBN 0 7153 2201 X

Printed in Singapore by KHL
for David & Charles
Brunel House   Newton Abbot   Devon

**Produced for David & Charles by
OutHouse Publishing**
Shalbourne, Marlborough, Wiltshire SN8 3QJ

For OutHouse Publishing:
Design and Picture Research Julian Holland
Editorial Manager Sue Gordon
Design Assistance Shane O'Dwyer, Nigel White
Maps and Pictograms Ethan Danielson

For David & Charles:
Commissioning Editor Mic Cady
Art Editor Alison Myer
Desk Editor Louise Crathorne
Production Controller Beverley Richardson

David & Charles books are available from all good bookshops;
alternatively you can contact our Orderline on (0)1626 334555
or write to us at FREEPOST EX2 110, David & Charles Direct,
Newton Abbot, TQ12 4ZZ (no stamp required UK mainland).

Visit our website at www.davidandcharles.co.uk

Along
Country Lines

EXPLORING THE RURAL RAILWAYS OF YESTERDAY

Paul Atterbury

D&C
David and Charles

CONTENTS

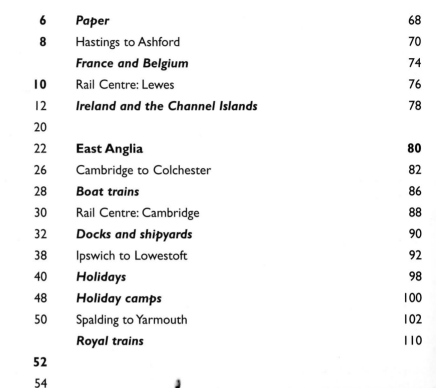

▼ Dressed in a smart New Look frock on a sunny day in July 1950, the wife of railway historian Patrick Whitehouse films a Manchester to Bournemouth express emerging from Chilcompton tunnel, in Somerset, double-headed by a pair of 0-6-0 freight locomotives.

EXPLORE THE SOUTH COAST WITH A DAY TOUR TICKET

AND ENJOY A DAY'S UNLIMITED TRAVEL

9'6 AREA 34 SECOND CLASS 8'6 AREA 35 SECOND CLASS

CHILDREN 3 and UNDER 14 YEARS, HALF PRICE

SUNDAYS to FRIDAYS 29 APRIL to 28 OCTOBER INCLUSIVE

DAY TOUR TICKETS ARE ON SALE AT ANY STATION OR TRAVEL AGENCY IN THE AREAS SHOWN OVERLEAF. THEY ARE AVAILABLE FOR TRAVEL BY ANY TRAIN ON THE DAY OF ISSUE WITHIN THE AREA SELECTED

SOUTHERN · A SUPPLEMENTARY CHARGE IS MADE FOR TRAVEL IN PULLMAN CARS

INTRODUCTION

At its peak, Britain's railway system included more than 20,000 miles of lines, a vast network whose tentacles reached into every corner of the country and whose connections made possible a vast choice of complicated cross-country journeys. Until the 1950s, passengers and freight depended on this network and the country railway was at the heart of the nation's business and social life. Within a decade everything had changed. Road transport was dominant and new economic policies resulted in the closure of thousands of miles of track. Hardest hit were the country lines; many parts of Britain lost not only their railways but also the life that went with them. Some country railways were spared, and those included in this book offer an incomparable vision of Britain's landscape, history and culture, to be enjoyed from the comfort of a modern train. Also included in the book is a selection of long-closed lines, brought to life by old photographs, postcards, leaflets and modern images of relics of the railway and its structures that may still be found in the landscape. Feature spreads illustrate and document many aspects of life on the country railway; some focus on country towns that were once busy rail centres.

Hunting for lost lines can be exciting and entertaining. An Ordnance Survey map is needed, as these mark the visible traces of lost railways. Sometimes trackbeds are easily seen and can often be explored from nearby roads. Some have become official footpaths or cycleways. Others have completely vanished. A keen eye for the lie of the land will make railway spotting easy. Embankments are often obvious, even if overgrown. Sometimes bridges and other structures survive in the fields and woods. Occasionally it is only a line of characteristic concrete fenceposts that gives the game away. Remember that many lost lines are now on private land, so permission to explore should always be sought from the landowner.

▲ Nothing brings the golden age of the country railway to life as effectively as old labels, tickets, leaflets and notices, particularly when they reflect the style and character of the original operating companies. For the collector, they represent living history. Items such as this SR luggage label are still readily available.

▲ For over a century the country railway was at the heart of our culture. Everything depended upon it, and everything travelled on it. As a result, railways provoked a great variety of humorous and sentimental images, particularly in the early years of the 20th century. Typical is this group of dogs, haughty but worried, with the caption: Missed the Connection.

► The heyday of the country railway was coincidental with that of the picture postcard. Cards offer modern readers an easy way to explore destinations great and small. All the holidaymakers in this Edwardian view of Bournemouth would probably have travelled to that resort by train.

Bournemouth from Pier

▼ Old photographs capture the spirit of the country railway and are rich in evocative detail. They are a reminder that even rural and remote routes were often busy. Here, at Builth Road in the summer of 1964, members of a train crew enjoy the sunshine on the platform prior to their tour of duty.

ABOUT THIS BOOK

Key to map of routes (see opposite page)

The route maps

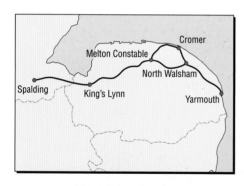

Each route has a simple map, to locate it within the country and to identify the principal places along the journey. Connecting lines and non-railway features are not shown.

▲ An enthusiastic rail traveller plans his journey.

The pictograms

Each route is introduced by a series of pictograms, as shown below, designed to indicate at a glance to both the railway enthusiast and the general reader the status or nature of the route and its particular character or features.

 Line open as part of the national network

 Line closed

 Preserved line

 Exceptionally scenic line

 Line with notable railway structures

 Part of the line now an official walking trail

 Part of the line now an official cycle route

 Not relevant to this route

HESKETH HUBBARD

The West Country

WEST OF EXETER

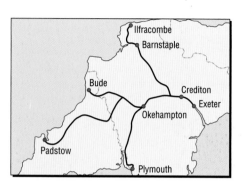

The London & South Western Railway was formed in June 1839, with its interests focused on Southampton and Portsmouth. When it was finally absorbed into the Southern Railway in 1923, it was operating trains over 966 miles of track. Much of this was measured in a huge network of suburban lines to the south and south-west of London, but there were also several long-distance routes. The most significant connected Waterloo with far away Devon and Cornwall, a line that ran deep into the heart of traditional GWR territory. The LSWR's progress westwards was slow and steady, from Basingstoke to Salisbury, from Salisbury to Yeovil and onwards to Exeter, which it reached in 1860. Meanwhile, in the 1850s work had started on a line northwards from Exeter to Barnstaple, along a route contested by the LSWR and the GWR.

▶ In July 1964, with the network nearing its end, an old Southern Railway locomotive hauls the Padstow section of the Atlantic Coast Express into Delabole. The bleak nature of the north Cornwall landscape can be clearly seen, along with the edge of the vast Delabole slate quarry. Slate quarrying was, and still is, a large-scale local industry and it benefited enormously from the coming of the railway in the 1880s.

▼ When the LSWR reached Exeter in 1860 it built itself a new station, initially named Queen Street and later Central. It was, and still is, much better placed for the city than the GWR's St David's, to which it is connected by a steeply curving link line. Much simplified in layout, Exeter Central now has a smart 1930s classical façade.

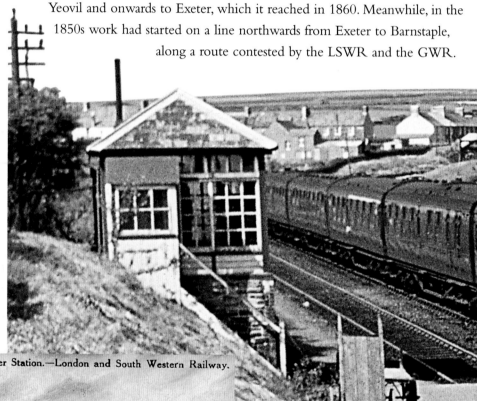

Exeter Station.—London and South Western Railway.

▶ The LSWR was always keen to promote itstelf and its services and it issued many postcards in the Edwardian era depicting its famous trains on its major routes. This one shows the American Boat Express, a scheduled boat train service connecting Waterloo and Plymouth.

► This early 1900s view of Crediton station reveals its mixed origins: the wide-hipped roofs are the mark of the early GWR. In fact, this was originally a GWR station, built by the broad-gauge Bristol & Exeter Railway to Brunel's plans.

▼ The descent into Ilfracombe from Morthoe was sharp and steep, so departing trains often had to be double-headed. Here both locomotives are Southern Region stock, but sometimes pairings of former SR and GWR locomotives could be seen, reflecting the diversity of trains serving the resort.

No. 31A.

SOUTHERN RAILWAY

October 4th, 1943, to April 30th, 1944, both dates inclusive.

TRAIN SERVICE AND FARES

BETWEEN

LONDON (Waterloo)

AND

EXETER

BARNSTAPLE JCT.

BIDEFORD (for Clovelly, Appledore and Westward Ho !)

TORRINGTON

BRAUNTON (for Saunton Sands and Croyde Bay)

MORTEHOE (for Woolacombe) and

ILFRACOMBE (for Combe Martin)

E. J. MISSENDEN, General Manager.

Waterlow & Sons Ltd., London & Dunstable.

T.W. 4003/$\frac{7,000}{13/9/43}$.

14

In the end the LSWR won it, and pushed onwards to Bideford and to Ilfracombe, which it reached in 1874. Another line went westwards from a junction north of Crediton to Okehampton and thence to Plymouth via Tavistock. There was also a long arm to Bude, on the north Cornwall coast. The next link in this complex West Country chain, from Halwill on the Bude line to Wadebridge and Padstow via Launceston, was built slowly as the North Cornwall Railway, between 1882 and 1899. The final piece of the jigsaw was a connecting line northwards from Halwill to Bideford via Torrington, and this had to wait until 1925, by which time the LSWR had disappeared into the Southern Railway. The LSWR's network west of Exeter was, in some ways, an ambitious folly. It competed with the GWR on its own territory, but at great cost. Much of it served a remote and underpopulated region, with little industry, apart from stone and slate quarries. The most useful parts were the main line to Plymouth and the long north Devon line to Ilfracombe, with holiday traffic on the latter well established before the end of the 19th century. Indeed, Ilfracombe was soon receiving trains from Exeter, Bristol and the Midlands via the long GWR branch to Barnstaple from Taunton.

When the Southern Railway took over this extended and rambling empire in 1923, it decided to make the most of it. The emphasis was on holiday traffic, so the Atlantic

▲ When photographed in 1974, Ilfracombe station was still standing and, though derelict, relatively intact. Now not a vestige remains, and the site is completely lost under new industrial development.

Coast Express came into the picture. Departing daily from Waterloo, this was a complex train made up of sections, each for a different destination west of Exeter. The main component went to Barnstaple and Ilfracombe, other parts ended up at Bude and Padstow. By comparison, the GWR's rival Cornish Riviera Express was a simple affair. Yet during the interwar years the Atlantic Coast Express enjoyed both considerable popularity and a great reputation, and it continued to run through the British Rail era of the 1950s and on to the 1960s, by which time it was a tired and elderly relic. It all came to an end in 1966 with the closure of the whole of the LSWR's network west of Exeter, except for the line to Barnstaple, reduced now to a truncated branch. Some freight services survived a bit longer but in essence the West Country was back where it started, in the arms of the GWR.

SURF RIDING, CROOKLETS BEACH, BUDE.

◄ Famous for its long sandy beaches and Atlantic rollers, Bude was the ideal holiday destination for many families in the interwar period. This 1936 postcard of Crooklets Beach, Bude, shows early surfboarders, and some splendid bathing costumes.

► The north Cornwall line was a late arrival on the railway map and had a relatively short life. Much of it was single-tracked. Yet the trackbed is still easily traced through the bleak and remote landscape, even though nature has often taken over. Near Port Isaac Road the curve of the trackbed through the cutting is clearly delineated beneath the invading and impenetrable gorse.

▲ A number of stations survive on the old lines west of Exeter, and those that do have usually been converted into comfortable houses. Some have abandoned their railway history, while others, including this example at Ashbury, west of Okehampton, and easily seen from the nearby road bridge, maintain the railway connection by incorporating the platforms into the garden.

THE ROUTES TODAY

Tracing the various routes provides the mixture of pleasure and pain that comes with any railway exploration, but on a grander scale. Although sections have disappeared, most of the network can still be seen in the landscape, thanks to the bleak nature of much of the terrain. Viaducts, notably at Meldon and Holsworthy, bridges, embankments, stations and other railway buildings survive, but in certain places, for example at Halwill Junction or Ilfracombe, it is hard to believe that the railway ever existed. Large stretches of the route are private and inaccessible, whereas others have become footpaths and cycleways, both official and unofficial. The most famous cycle path is the Camel Trail, along the riverside trackbed from Wadebridge to Padstow, and up into the hills to Wenford Bridge. In other places railway life has returned: a narrow-gauge line at Launceston, restored stations at Bideford and Torrington, both of which are on a cycleway, and the magnificent rebuilt Okehampton station, now receiving tourist trains again. There are museums and local collections, and in many places it is possible to re-live the history of the railway, or at least experience the lasting impact of it on the landscape and the communities it served. And from Exeter St David's real trains continue run to Barnstaple, across the hills and valleys of north Devon, along a line that lingers on, constantly under threat of closure but still offering the classic country railway journey, interspersed with echoes of past grandeur.

▶ In the early 1900s, when this card was published, Padstow was a small fishing village with a tidal quay used by local trading vessels. It developed significantly after the arrival of the railway and began a new life as a holiday resort. Today the place is thriving, although the railway is long gone, and the peace and quiet suggested by the card is no more than a distant memory.

▼ In the autumn of 1959 an ancient former LSWR locomotive lumbers over the iron girder bridge at Little Petherick Creek on its way to Padstow with a local stopping train. Today train and track have gone but the bridge survives as a landmark on the Camel Trail, one of England's premier trackbed cycleways and a delightful way to explore the Camel estuary between Padstow and Wadebridge.

The Quay, Padstow

PEOPLE

UNLIKE OTHER FORMS of transport, the train has an enduring and universal appeal. As small children, we were held up by our parents to watch passing trains; we bring up our own children on books illustrated with the kinds of trains they may never see. The excitement of the child standing on the station, getting on the train and travelling, or just standing by the track and waving, is palpable. Many adults retain some aspect of that enthusiasm, without necessarily becoming dedicated railway enthusiasts. Drawings by artists such as Thomas Rowlandson, in the early 1800s, reveal that even at the dawn of railway history the lure of the train was intense. For the Victorians the train was the wonder of the age, and millions of people who before had never left their village were now travelling far and wide, experiencing the pleasures, and pitfalls, of the ever-expanding railway network. Today trains, like cars, tend to look the same. They are a quick and relatively efficient means of travel, but they seem to lack the character of the trains of the past, trains now surrounded by an aura of romance and nostalgia. Yet people everywhere still stand and watch, and trains continue to work their magic.

▲ The railway lies at the heart of modern culture, and its appeal is wide-ranging. The trains are merely one element in the picture; it is the station that is the focal point. Excitement, boredom, romance, drama, comedy and tragedy are all part of the station experience. People are born, get married and die on stations, so why shouldn't they play music?

▲ Parents have from time immemorial held their tiny children up to watch passing trains, part of the complex process of learning to enjoy the train as part of the landscape. Not many people hold children up to watch traffic on the motorway. In the summer of 1970 this woman and her child, seated on a lock gate on the then derelict Kennet & Avon canal in Wiltshire, watch the Riviera Limited pass by.

▶ The lure of steam has always been irresistible to all ages, regardless of the size of locomotive, as this 1930s photo indicates.

▶ In his quest for a new approach to a familiar subject, the photographer has told these boys to hold up the sagging station sign at Danzey, north of Stratford-on-Avon.

◀ Part of the appeal of locomotives is the fact that they have, and have always had, names. Somehow, a number is not enough. Perhaps it was this that prompted these children to write names on the dusty body of an otherwise anonymous diesel locomotive. They have chosen well: there have been 18 locomotives called 'Samson' and eight named 'Odin'.

TAUNTON TO BARNSTAPLE

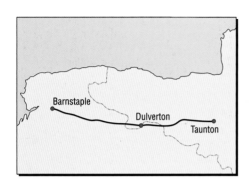

On 1 November 1873 the first train from Taunton steamed slowly into the newly completed wooden terminus buildings to the east of Barnstaple's town centre, a station known as Barnstaple Victoria Road. This was the culmination of a railway scheme first authorized in 1864, and it had taken nearly ten years to construct the 43 miles required. The builder was the Devon & Somerset Railway, an independent company backed by the Bristol & Exeter, who were keen to push their broad-gauge network westwards into north Devon. In effect a long branch line, it was cheaply built and initially had only three passing points. Services were, as a result, chaotic, but things improved in 1881 when it was all converted to standard gauge. Six years later a short spur was opened to link it to Barnstaple Junction, the terminus station of the LSWR's line from Exeter. The inspiration for this was the railway from Barnstaple to Ilfracombe, completed in 1874, which had brought rapid growth and much holiday traffic to that north Devon resort. This spur enabled trains from Taunton, and thus from many parts of central Britain, to run through to Ilfracombe. At this point the GWR, keen to expand its holiday and freight traffic at the expense of its great rival, the LSWR, took an interest and in 1901 bought the Devon & Somerset company. Later improvements allowed GWR trains to bypass Victoria Road, with the result that traffic to the station diminished and it was eventually closed and demolished. By this time, centrally placed Barnstaple Town had been the main station for some years, so Victoria Road was in any case redundant.

Apart from the holiday trains, the only traffic of any significance was that servicing the needs of local agriculture, including the carriage of both cattle and rabbits. The

▲ Taunton can be identified from many directions by its great church tower, as this card makes clear. The station is away from the town centre but there are views over the town from westbound trains going towards the junction by Norton Fitzwarren, where the lines to Minehead and to Barnstaple branched away. The Minehead line survives as a preserved railway.

▲ The Devon & Somerset was essentially a local line serving remote areas, and built rather slowly with a small budget. However, the landscape demanded some comparatively expensive engineering, including large river bridges. Today the iron girders are long gone but stone support pillars or approach arches survive. This, looking like some overgrown medieval ruin, is the approach arch to the former crossing of the Exe.

◄ Wiveliscombe station was the second stop on the line and the station was, for once, fairly near the little town it served. On a late summer's afternoon in 1963 the Barnstaple train pulls in. Although closure is threatening, the station is still looking tidy.

single-track line took a rural route that managed to avoid most of the villages and small towns along the way. Dulverton and South Molton, the only places of substance, were both some distance from the railway, and most of the other intermediate stations served small and remote villages. The landscape is hilly, cut by deep river valleys, so some expensive engineering was required, including three tunnels and substantial iron girder bridges over the Mole, the Exe and the Tone. Construction may have been done cheaply, but care was taken with finish and detailing, notably frequent use of rough-cut local stone. It was a leisurely, delightful journey through a lovely landscape, with distant views of Exmoor. However, that was not enough to generate significant income and it was really only the holiday traffic to Ilfracombe and other north Devon resorts that kept the line open. Closure was inevitable, and it finally came in October 1966.

THE ROUTE TODAY

Sections of the old railway line have been lost to farming, road building and into people's back gardens, and many bridges have gone, but some handsome stone stations and other buildings survive, notably at Dulverton. Considerably altered, by contrast, is the site of Morebath Junction, from where a short connecting branch ran south to Tiverton via Bampton, allowing access to north Devon from Exeter and the south. Sadly, much of the route is today relatively inaccessible and private, though it can easily be identified and followed from minor roads. Comparatively apparent are sections that have been taken over as farm access tracks. The landscape is constantly appealing and varied as the line winds its way through the hills; it would make a glorious long-distance footpath. Inevitably, the rural and remote nature of the line has meant that many sections are overgrown and impenetrable, but those that are accessible have a distinct sense of hidden mystery, heightened by the usual elements that identify any lost railway, such as concrete fence posts, old wooden gates and traces of platelayers' huts. However, deep in the peaceful Devon countryside, it is hard to visualize those holiday expresses charging by.

▲ Dulverton was a substantial station with extensive freight facilities including a large goods shed. However, as this 1963 photograph suggests, it was a long way from the town. Today, the main station building, the goods shed and some of the platforms survive, along with an old railway hotel that has been converted into apartments.

◀ The railway has left its mark on the glorious landscape. Here, its route can be identified in the middle distance as a straight line of trees along the valley of the Yeo, with the hills around Molland in the distance.

▶ The end of the line, literally, at Barnstaple Victoria Road, the former terminus of the Devon & Somerset Railway: closure is imminent, and even the station name board is falling apart.

CLAY

CLAY DEPOSITS in Purbeck, in Dorset, and north Devon have been exploited for centuries but it was not until the early 1800s that railways were used to transport the clay from the pits to the harbours. Extensive networks of narrow- and standard-gauge lines were developed in the Victorian era, and these continued to flourish at least until the 1960s, serving harbours such as Poole, in Dorset, and Fremington, in north Devon, from where the clay was shipped to other British and European ports. This traffic had finished by the early 1980s. In many parts of Britain, but on a much more localized basis, brickmakers also used the railways to transport clay in bulk from the pits to the brickworks.

More significant, and very much alive today, is Cornwall's china clay industry, which has flourished since the late 18th century, when the deposits were first discovered. The first china clay railway opened in 1829 from St Austell to Pentewan harbour, and by the 1850s a large network

▲ Most brickworks were adjacent to huge clay pits, many of which were railway-operated. Typical was Southam, near Rugby, where the 1903 locomotive 'Jurassic' was still at work in 1954 hauling clay hoppers. Now preserved, 'Jurassic' lives at the Bala Lake Railway.

▼ Clay is still a major bulk cargo for independent freight railways. Here at the loading complex at Treviscoe a class 66 locomotive in EWS colours is ready to depart.

of lines had been developed around St Blazey, the centre of the industry, with connections to the south coast harbours of Par and Fowey. Expansion continued, partly to satisfy the ever-increasing demands of the papermaking industry and the Staffordshire potteries and partly to develop the massive export trade that is still the major area of the china clay business. For decades now, china clay trains have run regularly between Cornwall and Stoke-on-Trent.

Until 1982 wooden wagons with distinctive hoods were a memorable feature of these trains, but now modern bogie hoppers are used, carrying up to 700,000 tons per year. However, today the bulk of the china clay traffic is short haul, to Fowey harbour for export.

▲ Despite the loss of passenger services decades ago, Fowey is still a busy rail centre, servicing the clay trade. China clay from the massive deposits in Cornwall, used in papermaking, pharmaceuticals and many other industries as well as ceramics, is a major export cargo. Here, in the 1980s, a train of Fowey-bound clay wagons passes through Golant.

▼ South Devon supported an extensive ceramics industry through much of the 19th and 20th centuries, thanks to local clay deposits. Many potteries, including the pipe works adjacent to Heathfield station, to the north of Newton Abbot, used the railways for the transportation of raw materials and finished products.

RAIL CENTRE: BARNSTAPLE

TODAY BARNSTAPLE is a rather tired, single-tracked station at the end of the long branch line from Exeter. It is some way from the town centre and, despite various marketing ploys aimed at improving usage, notably naming it The Tarka Line, the Barnstaple branch faces an uncertain future.

It was not always thus. Up until the closures of the 1960s, Barnstaple had three stations, offering journeys in five directions and connections to several other stations. The town's first railway, a horse-drawn tramway, opened in 1848 but connections to the national network did not come until the 1870s, when the Great Western opened its line from Taunton to Victoria Road station, and the London & South Western its line from Exeter to Barnstaple Junction (today's Barnstaple station). A new bridge over the Taw enabled the Town station to be built on the river's north bank and opened up the way to Ilfracombe, a resort much developed from then on by holiday traffic. When it opened in 1898, the Lynton & Barnstaple Railway also used the Town station. Finally, in 1925 the line south to Torrington was opened through to Halwill Junction, where it met the main line from Okehampton to Bude, with connections to Padstow.

Bideford from Fort

BIDEFORD
Famous for its potteries, its shipyards, its quays and its transatlantic trade, which flourished until the 19th century, Bideford was settling into its new life as a tourist town when the railway arrived. This postcard, which shows the town, the Torridge and its famous 24-arch bridge, was written in 1916 by a soldier to his girl in London. 'Ireland Sat. worse luck', he says. The station, now restored as a tourist attraction, was just to the left of the picture.

Exeter
The Cathedral

EXETER
This romantic postcard view of the cathedral, which dates from the 12th century, was posted in 1907. Then, as now, the train from Barnstaple came into St David's, the earliest of Exeter's three stations. Each was built by a different railway company. The first company to reach the city was the Bristol & Exeter (later part of the GWR) in 1844, followed by the South Devon, which opened St Thomas' station in 1846. Both were Brunel enterprises. The rival LSWR built Exeter Central (originally called Queen Street) in 1860. This was later joined to St David's, with the result that even today trains for London leave St David's in two different directions. Central station is best located for exploring the city.

ILFRACOMBE

Ilfracombe's popularity as a resort, thanks to its cliff setting and its beaches, increased enormously after the coming of the railway in 1874. Its heyday was probably the 1920s and 1930s, when holiday expresses came directly to the town from London, the Midlands and other parts of Britain. This postcard shows the resort in the early 1900s. The beaches, promenades and cliff walks are crowded, a paddlesteamer is arriving, some comedians are performing (to empty seats), flags are flying on the cliff top and everyone is enjoying the sun. The sender of the card, writing to his mother in August 1905, says, 'This is a beautiful spot. Nothing but hills and vales.' The station, now buried under an industrial estate, was set high above the town.

A goods train on the Taw viaduct, 1950s

BARNSTAPLE

LYNMOUTH

The popularity of Lynton and Lynmouth, and the cliff railway that links them, was assured with the opening of the narrow-gauge Lynton & Barnstaple, which from 1898 to 1935 wound its slow, scenic way through the north Devon hills to that hitherto remote stretch of coast. Now there are plans to reopen it. This card shows Lynmouth's pretty riverside before it was devastated by floods in 1953.

Bridge Street, Taunton

TAUNTON

The GWR line from Taunton to Barnstaple, in reality a long branch, allowed the Great Western into a rival company's territory. It also, ultimately, enabled the GWR to gain a share of the Ilfracombe and north Devon holiday traffic. Taunton's first station opened in 1842, on a site well to the north of the town. Later it was much expanded and became an important rail centre itself, offering routes in six directions. Posted in 1909, this view of Bridge Street, one of the town's main thoroughfares, is full of period detail: smart, well-dressed people, a tramcar, street lighting, delivery carts, a lady driving in a donkey cart with her dog, and interesting shops, one of which offers petrol for sale (there were no garages yet).

DINING AND SLEEPING

British Railways

U NTIL THE 1870s refreshments were only available from stations, and stops on the journey were often chaotic as passengers struggled to eat or buy supplies for the journey. The development of corridor-connected carriages made restaurant cars possible. The first example was a modified American-style Pullman introduced by the Great Northern Railway in 1879. Other companies quickly followed and soon specially built restaurant and kitchen cars were in widespread use. Many restaurant cars had a bar area, but more informal buffet cars appeared from 1899. The heyday of the restaurant car was probably from the 1920s to the 1960s, when they were attached as a matter of course to many services, and were available to different classes of ticket holders. It was at this point that the railway breakfast became a famous part of the British train experience. Today, few railway companies operate a full restaurant car service with on-board cooking and most passengers have to put up with bar service or the ubiquitous trolley. The self-contained sleeping car, with individual berths, proper bedding and lavatory facilities, first appeared in 1873, and then became universal on longer routes.

PASSENGER TRAVEL
FACILITIES

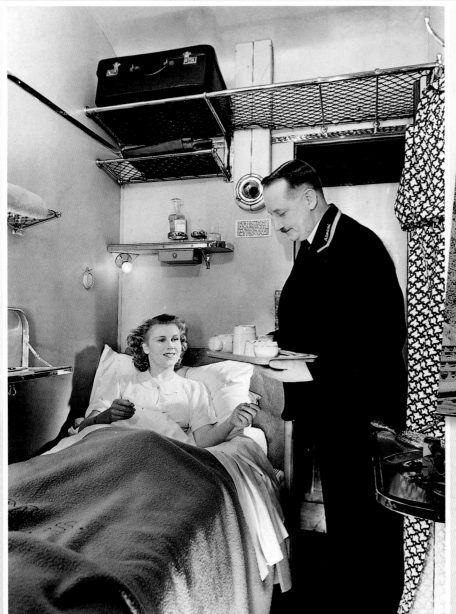

The Hungry Traveller

▲ The Hungry Traveller, issued by British Railways in the late 1950s, promoted all rail catering facilities, including station refreshment rooms and bars, restaurant cars, and pre-packed meal and picnic boxes.

◀ In 1946, as train travel returned to normal after World War II, British Railways began to promote its sleeper services. This delightful image shows a uniformed attendant delivering early morning tea to a first class passenger who looks remarkably fresh and *soignée*.

◀ Luncheon is being served in the third-class restaurant and bar car on a GWR train out of London in 1946.

▶ At the time this card was issued by the LNWR in about 1910, to promote its boat train service to Liverpool for travellers to America, kitchen cars were equipped with coal-fired stoves. The risk of fire encouraged a general move to kitchens using bottled gas and electricity from the 1920s onwards.

THE KITCHEN.
L. & N. W. AMERICAN SPECIAL.

BRISTOL TO WEYMOUTH

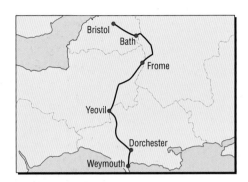

The Beeching axe was very thorough in its reduction of Britain's railway network in the 1960s, but there were some surprising survivors. One such is the line from Bristol to Weymouth, a meandering and predominantly rural route that must have looked like a prime candidate for closure. Somehow it escaped and is now one of the best country railways in England, offering a leisurely exploration of some of the more secret parts of south-western Britain.

Linking Somerset, Wiltshire and Dorset, the line has a long history, its route having been planned by the Wiltshire, Somerset & Weymouth Railway in 1845. This grandly named company was nominally independent but its backer was the GWR, keen to gain access to a south coast port, and thus to French and Channel Islands' traffic. It was planned from the start as a broad-gauge line, part of Brunel's ever-expanding empire, and the first section opened in

TRAMWAYS CENTRE, BRISTOL   37592

▲ There is no tram to be seen in this 1930s view of Tramways Centre, at the heart of Bristol, but it is full of period detail. Traffic is somewhat lighter than today, but otherwise the scene is still recognizable. The gothic splendour of Temple Meads station is a suitable starting point for a notably old-fashioned journey. The train usually departs from a platform resplendent with the stylish cream and brown GWR ceramic signage of the 1930s.

▶ The ubiquitous modern diesel railcars operate the Bristol to Weymouth service today, but sometimes in the summer longer locomotive-hauled trains are used to cope with the holiday traffic. This view of the train passing Claverton Weir, near Bath, shows the quality of landscape associated with the route.

◄ A stopping train from Salisbury to Bristol, under the control of a GWR Hall locomotive, pauses at Bradford-on-Avon in 1963, having joined the Bristol to Weymouth line at Westbury. For much of its life, this route was kept busy with traffic generated by its various connections with other main lines. Typical were the summer holiday expresses that linked Weymouth directly with the Midlands and the North via this route.

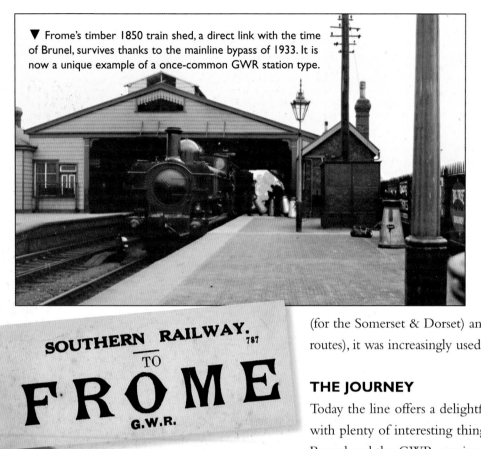

▼ Frome's timber 1850 train shed, a direct link with the time of Brunel, survives thanks to the mainline bypass of 1933. It is now a unique example of a once-common GWR station type.

SOUTHERN RAILWAY. 787
TO
FROME
G.W.R.

1848. Things then began to go wrong and construction was constantly delayed by difficulties and financial problems. In 1851 the GWR ran out of patience and took over what remained of the WS&WR, finally completing the line in 1857. It remained a broad-gauge route until 1874, and in 1884 it was converted to double track. By 1876 the GWR was operating shipping services from Weymouth. Apart from access to Weymouth harbour, there were other advantages for the owners, and thanks to its connections with main lines at Westbury (for GWR West Country services), Bruton (for the Somerset & Dorset) and Yeovil (for the LSWR's West of England routes), it was increasingly used by freight and holiday traffic.

THE JOURNEY

Today the line offers a delightful journey of great landscape diversity, with plenty of interesting things to see en route. Elements reflecting Brunel and the GWR survive and many stations are old-fashioned in atmosphere. Some are request stops, so passengers wanting to board the train have to stand on the platform and wave. Those on the train have

◀ At Castle Cary the Weymouth train leaves the GWR main line for the now single-tracked route southwards through the hills of Dorset, a notably remote region where stations that elsewhere would have closed years ago survive as request stops.

▲ In the 1950s a long Weymouth-bound holiday train, headed by a GWR Hall locomotive, waits at Yeovil Pen Mill station. Journey's end is now in sight for weary passengers who have travelled for hours from the north of England. At this point there were connections for Yeovil's other stations, Town and Junction. With semaphore signals intact, Pen Mill looks remarkably similar today.

to ask the guard in advance to arrange for it to stop. Old semaphore signals are still in use in some areas, and other echoes of past railway life are to be seen.

The journey starts from Bristol Temple Meads and the train follows the main line to Bath before turning south along the Avon valley to Bradford. It crosses the wide, open Wiltshire landscape to Trowbridge and Westbury, a windswept station dominated by the massive stone traffic from nearby quarries. The next stretch is along the GWR main line to Exeter, via Frome, Bruton and Castle Cary, where the Weymouth line turns south through the gentle hills and farmland of Somerset to Yeovil, a town that has two of its original three stations still in use, albeit not connected by scheduled services. The train now enters the glorious and remote hill country of Dorset, running south through villages redolent of Thomas Hardy and over the territory of once-famous hunts to Maiden Newton, formerly the junction for the branch line to Bridport and West Bay, another creation of the GWR's south coast harbour ambitions.

Maiden Newton Railway Station

◄ As so often in early 20th-century postcards, everyone is posing for the camera. This is Maiden Newton in about 1910. The station is not greatly changed today, except that it now has no staff and not many trains. To the left of the footbridge was the bay platform for the Bridport branch, a line that somehow kept going until the mid-1970s.

▼ The Weymouth harbour tramway was a delightful anachronism and until its closure in the late 1980s trains wound their way through the traffic and the holidaymakers. It was built to serve the ferries to France and the Channel Islands, and in this typical 1960s view a boat train of SR stock, hauled by a GWR tank locomotive, sets off along the crowded quayside towards the town centre. Perhaps those on the train have taken part in one of the excursions advertised in the booklet on the right.

Dorchester, another two-station town, is approached through Poundbury tunnel, which was dug instead of a cutting, on Brunel's orders, to preserve the Iron Age earthworks above. In Dorchester the rails of the GWR and the LSWR come together, to share the final few miles down to Weymouth. The two lines opened on the same day in 1857, a reflection of the cooperation between the two companies that continued until the era of British Railways. From Weymouth they built a joint extension to serve Portland, initially for both broad and standard gauge, and there were equally equitable arrangements about the use of the Weymouth harbour tramway, whose route through the town centre to the quayside ferry port was in use until the late 1980s. In its heyday Weymouth, the meeting point for all kinds of GWR and SR locomotives and vehicles, was a trainspotter's dream.

▲ The line from Weymouth to Dorchester, used by both GWR and SR trains, was heavily graded, so double-heading was common. Here, in the summer of 1939, as war clouds were gathering, a long express crawls past Upwey Wishing Well Halt.

Weymouth. The Bay.

◀ Weymouth has been a resort since the 18th century, thanks to its harbour and sheltered sandy beaches, but it was the railway that really made the town famous. This Edwardian card gives the flavour of the beach, complete with bathing machines.

DAY EXCURSIONS
By sea
FROM WEYMOUTH

CHANNEL ISLANDS
Guernsey and Jersey
FRANCE Cherbourg
No Passport

1962

SOUTHERN
BRITISH RAILWAYS

MAIL AND PARCELS

BY AN 1838 ACT OF Parliament the Postmaster General was empowered to require any railway company to carry the mail. The same year saw the introduction of the first travelling post offices, mobile sorting offices initially converted from horse boxes. The service grew rapidly. By the 1850s dedicated mail trains were in use and from 1882 post boxes were fitted to mail trains. Parcel post was carried by train from the early 1880s. By the 1860s the automatic exchange of mailbags between the trackside and a moving train had been perfected, and by 1911 there were 245 locations where this could take place. By 1967 only 34 remained, and the system was last used in 1971. The layout of the vehicles, with sorting boxes on one side and hooks for mail bags on the other, changed little during the life of the travelling post offices (TPOs). In recent times, with more mail and parcels going by road, the number of TPOs began to diminish. In the early 1990s London was still handling 68 trains a day, but there was then a rapid decline and the mail trains stopped in 2004.

▲ In 1967 some mail trains were still steam-hauled, including this one, heading north near Tebay on the West Coast main line. The water troughs, for automatically filling the tanks in the locomotive's tender, are still in place between the tracks.

◄ This LNWR official postcard from the Edwardian era shows the company's latest travelling post office, complete with apparatus for collecting and discharging mail bags at speed.

Postmen of the British Empire:
the Night Mail Train,
A.D. 1904

◄ 'Postmen of the British Empire' was the title of a series of postcards issued in 1904 depicting postal services around the empire. This one shows mail bags being loaded prior to the departure of the Night Mail from some British city. Mail was carried on many passenger trains, as well as on the dedicated mail trains and travelling post offices.

▼ Mail bags piled up on trolleys on the platform and awaiting the train used to be a common sight on stations all over Britain, but this is now a distant memory. Pictured here, in 1964, is Glastonbury & Street station, where the mail bags would have been loaded onto the train for Evercreech Junction for onward transport to a regional sorting office or TPO.

SHREWSBURY
2 NOV
1981

SHREWSBURY-YORK T.P.O.

► ▲ The process of sorting the mail on a TPO did not change from its inception in early Victorian days until the last services were withdrawn in 2004. This shows the sorters on the regular Shrewsbury to York service. Above is an example of the special TPO postmark, used on letters posted in the box that was attached to the carriage.

BATH TO BOURNEMOUTH

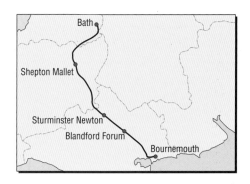

Old railway lines are a bit like football teams: some are very well known and attract an army of enthusiasts, while others are so obscure they seem to have precious few supporters. The process seems to be arbitrary and often has more to do with emotion and nostalgia than geography or history. Always high in anyone's premier league of old railways is the Somerset & Dorset, and the magic initials S&DJR will ensure high prices among collectors of railway memorabilia.

The appeal of this particular railway is easy to understand. Throughout its life it managed to maintain a sense of independence, even into the days of British Railways. Unlike many main lines in the south-west of England, its route ran north to south, and through its connections it made possible journeys that crossed conventional regional boundaries. It was heavily engineered and steeply graded, so it always attracted hordes of railway enthusiasts keen to see, and hear, steam locomotives working really hard. For the same reason, it was well photographed, and many books have ensured its lasting popularity. Despite the high profile it enjoys today, the Somerset & Dorset was actually a comparatively small railway, with a chequered history.

▼ Bath Green Park was a busy terminus where trains from the Midlands and the North met those coming from the south coast. Here, in 1950, a long holiday express rests after the heavy haul across the Mendips. Soon fresh locomotives and crews will take it on to Mangotsfield and the North. Today the train shed houses shops and a supermarket.

Bath from Beechen Cliffs.

◄ The city of Bath, set in the valley of the Avon, can be seen from the hills to the south. This early postcard view gives a sense of the panorama, with the abbey, the Georgian terraces and the parks and gardens all visible. The main station is in the foreground.

SOUTHERN RAILWAY. (Stook, 94 U)

TO

S. & D. Rly.,

Via

In the 19th century Somerset was surprisingly well equipped with railways and the area between Taunton and Bristol was a mass of lines, many built to exploit the riches of the Somerset coalfields. However, few penetrated south of the frontier formed by the LSWR's main line from Salisbury to Exeter. In the 1850s and 1860s a couple of small companies began to change the pattern. First came the Somerset Central Railway, which built a small network linking Glastonbury with Highbridge, Burnham-on-Sea, Wells and Cole. Next, the Dorset Central Railway opened a line from Wimborne to Blandford. This was later extended northwards to Templecombe, where it met the LSWR's main line, and thence to Cole. In 1862 these two companies formed themselves into the Somerset & Dorset Railway, with the hope

▲ With closure imminent, the Somerset & Dorset route saw many specials, often long trains demanding skilful driving on the hilly line. Here, in 1965, driver Harold Burford uses all his experience as his train attacks the steep gradient from Bath Green Park.

◄ From Bath the line climbs rapidly and cuts its way through the hills in a sequence of tunnels. First was the Devonshire tunnel, whose steep gradient and narrow bore gave the footplate crew an unpleasant time, and an early test of their skills. Today it is sealed and inaccessible but the approach to the tunnel from the south is one of the S&D's magical hidden places.

▲ Snow used to be a frequent problem on the Mendips in winter, and the severe weather of 1963 closed the line for several days, hastening its end. Here, in January of that year, crews at Binegar struggle to clear the lines.

▲ In 1952 Mr Down, stationmaster at Binegar, poses for the S&D's most famous photographer, Ivo Peters, with the crew of a permanent way maintenance trolley.

of encouraging traffic from Bristol to the south coast via their lines and various connections. However, by 1870 the directors realized they had a railway that went nowhere in particular, and a financial crisis loomed. Bravely, they decided to rescue the whole edifice by building a new direct route northwards to Bath and Bristol.

Leaving the existing network at Evercreech, this carved its way northwards through the Mendips. It was completed at enormous expense in 1874, but the company was soon in trouble and in 1876 it was leased by its wealthier neighbours, the Midland and the LSWR, who could see the potential it offered. Re-launched as the Somerset & Dorset Joint Railway, it was soon carrying large quantities of freight and passenger traffic, despite the demanding nature of its route and the frequent need for double-heading and banking locomotives. It benefited from its many connections with other lines, at Bath, Radstock, Shepton Mallet,

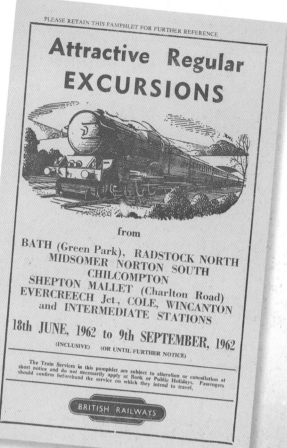

Attractive Regular EXCURSIONS

PLEASE RETAIN THIS PAMPHLET FOR FURTHER REFERENCE

from

BATH (Green Park), RADSTOCK NORTH
MIDSOMER NORTON SOUTH
CHILCOMPTON
SHEPTON MALLET (Charlton Road)
EVERCREECH Jct, COLE, WINCANTON
and INTERMEDIATE STATIONS

18th JUNE, 1962 to 9th SEPTEMBER, 1962
(INCLUSIVE) (OR UNTIL FURTHER NOTICE)

The Train Services in this pamphlet are subject to alteration or cancellation at short notice and do not necessarily apply at Bank or Public Holidays. Passengers should confirm beforehand the service on which they intend to travel.

BRITISH RAILWAYS

▲ The route of the Somerset & Dorset has many secret places that retain the magic of the railway. In the early 1990s, this autumnal view shows the approach to Winsor Hill tunnel, one of the few that is not locked and barred.

▼ Masbury Summit, the end of the long climb from Bath, was the place that drivers, and particularly firemen, longed to reach. In the summer of 1949 two old LMS locomotives have guided the Pines Express to this point, the start of the descent to Evercreech. The small boy engrossed by the passing train is Ivo Peters' son Julian.

◀ In many places the S&D has left a mark on the landscape that is little diminished by the passage of time and the encroachment of nature. In a field south of Binegar a farm accommodation bridge survives, along with a section of embankment, but the passage of trains seems centuries, rather than decades, ago.

Cole, Templecombe and Broadstone. In the late 19th century the S&D was enlarged, to cater for the extra traffic, and by the 1920s it had become a major holiday route, with a series of express services linking the resorts of the south coast with the industrial centres of the Midlands and the North. Best known was the Pines Express, which continued to run until the 1960s. The heavy freights and the holiday traffic diminished and by the mid-1960s only local services were keeping the Somerset & Dorset alive. The end came in March 1966, by which time much of the railway network in the counties of Somerset and Dorset had disappeared.

THE ROUTE TODAY

Since then, many things have happened. Large sections of the route have vanished back into the landscape, notably around Evercreech Junction, the famous meeting point of mainline expresses and local services to Wells, Glastonbury and Highbridge.

▼ From the late 19th century the S&D was a major freight route, and this traffic continued until the early 1960s. The sight of long freight trains hauled by some of the largest steam locomotives in use in Britain was one that always thrilled the enthusiast. Typical is the view of a long freight train crossing Prestleigh viaduct in 1955. After the line's closure, this viaduct was blown up.

◄ Even though Evercreech Junction station was in the middle of nowhere and a long way from its village, all trains stopped there, including the down Pines Express on 6 July 1959. It was a vital spot for taking water and for attaching or detaching banking engines.

▼ This 1952 photograph of Evercreech Junction station shows the famous railway historian O S Nock pointing out to his wife the line of locomotives waiting to bank trains on the long climb northwards over the Mendips. Today the station buildings survive but everything to the north of the station has vanished, including the junction itself.

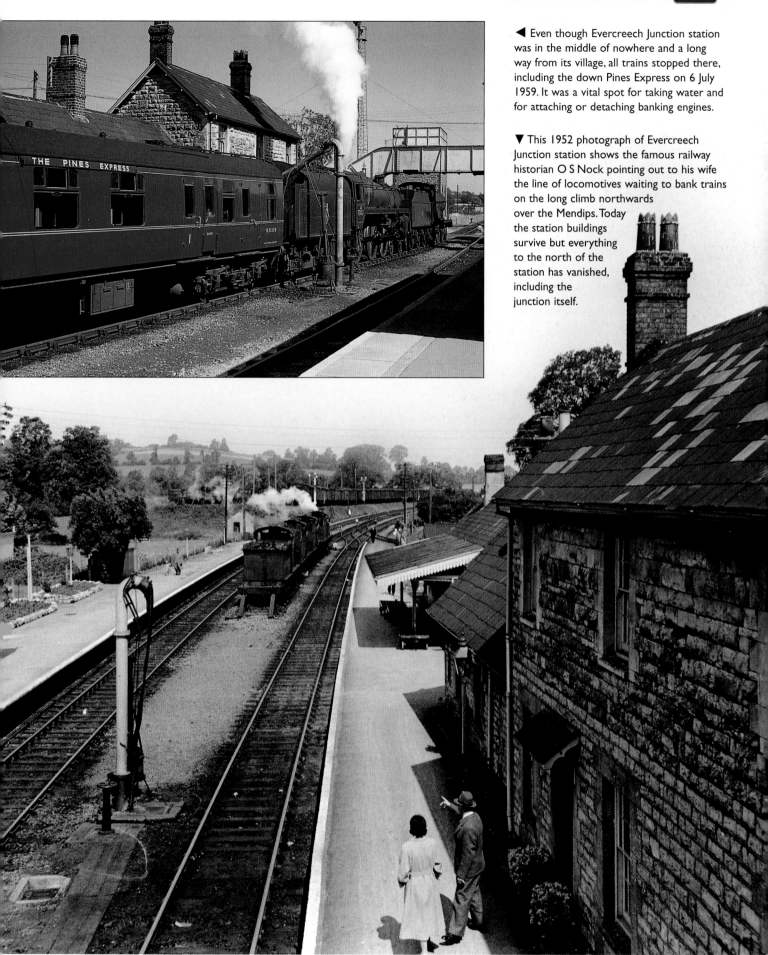

In other places the trackbed survives and is easily explored. The section north of Evercreech was heavily engineered and plenty remains to be seen in the way of tunnels, viaducts, bridges and embankments all the way to Bath. And in some quiet and hidden spots the old atmosphere of the S&D lingers on. Major viaducts include Charlton, near Shepton Mallet, and Midford and Tucking Mill, south of Bath. Stations and platforms remain, some as houses and gardens, others, for example Midsomer Norton and Shillingstone, brought back to a kind of railway life. Even Bath's Green Park terminus is still there, with its great train shed now housing a shopping centre. Sections of the line are official footpaths, but much of the route is still in private hands. However, the popularity of the S&D means that even in the most remote and private places there seem to be well-trodden paths. Exploring the remains of the S&D is clearly a national pastime. In fact, with the aid of a good map, it is possible to visit much of the route from minor roads and tracks without breaking the laws of trespass.

Inevitably, there are Somerset & Dorset societies and supporter groups, and through their efforts the line's history is kept alive. In some places the past is actually coming back to life and trains are running again on parts of the route. There is the Gartell Light Railway south of Templecombe, and things are moving in the Radstock area. Other plans are being drawn up. The S & D cannot die.

▲ Cole station was the original meeting point of the Somerset Central and the Dorset Central, the two companies that built much of the route in the 1860s. Passengers changed here for Bruton, on the GWR main line to Exeter. Like several other S&D stations, Cole was famous for its flower beds.

▼ Large sections of the S&D can be traced. South of Bruton the trackbed survives as a raised embankment, clearly defined in the landscape and now the province of cows rather than trains.

► This Edwardian postcard shows a busy scene at the LSWR station at Templecombe. It is likely that some of these passengers would have changed here from trains on the S&D line as this was the major interchange station on the route. Today Templecombe looks completely different, with just a single platform, a station building and a 1930s signal box.

◄ The Somerset & Dorset has always been a favourite among railway enthusiasts and the initials S&DJR on any artefact always excite collectors. There would be many queueing up to buy these buckets, even though hundreds must have been made.

▼ Bournemouth's West station was the end of the line for many trains on the S&D. From here or Branksome there were connections to other south coast resorts, including Weymouth and Swanage. As this postcard suggests, through the 1920s and the 1930s Bournemouth was a smart place and it attracted holidaymakers, most of whom travelled by train, from many parts of Britain.

THE PINE WALK. BOURNEMOUTH.

SIGNAL BOXES

THE SIGNAL BOX is a classic component of the railway landscape. In 1900 there were more than 13,000 all over Britain. Today, with electronic signalling almost universal, not many remain in use. The typical box emerged in the 1860s: two storeys, with the interlocking machinery on the ground floor and the levers and controls on the top floor, to give the signalman a good view. Styles varied from company to company and from region to region, but the lower part

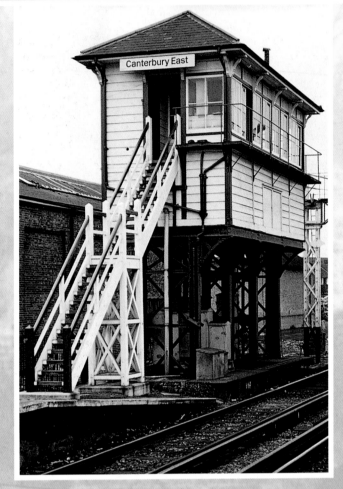

Canterbury East

◀ In 1958 at Old Ford, in east London, Joyce Wiltshire maintains a tradition started by women in wartime.

Vol.9 No.6 June 1958

British Railways Magazine 3d

London Midland Region

▲ Canterbury East, seen here in the 1980s, is unusual both because of its height and because it is carried on open iron latticework supports. In other details, such as the hipped roof, sash windows and railed gangway, it is typical.

tended to be of brick or stone and the upper part weather-boarded wood, often with barge-boarding or other detailing. Location often determined the design of the box: some are cantilevered, some are unusually tall, some are incorporated into a bridge. In the 1930s a modernist style emerged, with flat roofs and rounded corners. The Southern Railway was particularly keen on these. Most boxes had stoves and other creature comforts, for the signalman led an isolated life, working long hours.

◀ Denthead, on the Settle & Carlisle line, is a remote box in a glorious and wild landscape. Grabbing a moment between trains, the signalman has been to the oil store to refill the signal lamps.

▼ The massive, three-storey box at Severn Bridge Junction, Shrewsbury, is justly famous, its scale reflecting the complexity of traffic at Shrewsbury in its heyday. It stands between the Birmingham and the Hereford lines, a grand memorial to all signal boxes, everywhere.

▼ The first signal boxes were small structures on the station platform, simple shelters for the levers and machinery. This platform box at Milborne Port, near Sherborne in Dorset, is of a later date but reflects the style. As the notice indicates, it also served as a ticket office. Milborne Port station and its box were closed in the 1960s.

VIADUCTS

THE VIADUCT is the most dramatic of all railway structures, and the one that makes the most enduring impact on the landscape. All over Britain, long after the lines have been closed, many still stand. The engineering principles had been well understood for centuries, but nothing of any significant size was built in Britain until the railway age, when large viaducts, mostly of brick or stone, suddenly proliferated. Early examples include Stephenson's Sankey viaduct on the Liverpool & Manchester Railway, whose eight arches were completed in 1830, and Buck's 27-arched Stockport viaduct of 1842. In many cases viaducts were chosen in preference to embankments on grounds of cost and stability. In theory the number of arches could be unlimited. Britain's longest, at 1,275 yards, is the Welland in Rutland, completed in 1879. The best viaducts are defined by the height and curve of the arch and the thinness of the piers, and in many cases they achieve an elegance unusual in an engineering structure of such a scale. Brick and stone were the favoured materials, often used in conjunction with iron trusses. At first cast iron was employed but fears about stability inspired a switch to wrought iron from the late 1840s. Unusual was Brunel's use of timber for many viaducts in Devon and Cornwall, the last of which remained in service until 1934. Concrete, as blockwork or cast in situ, was used from the 1890s, with the 21 arches of Scotland's Glenfinnan being a particularly impressive example.

◀ Viaducts are a major feature of the line westwards from Plymouth to Penzance. Many were originally built from timber, to Brunel's designs, and from the late Victorian period onwards were gradually replaced. Today, their diversity, in terms of structure as well as landscape setting, adds greatly to the pleasures of the journey. Here, a modern Virgin train crosses the Largin viaduct.

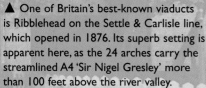

▲ One of Britain's best-known viaducts is Ribblehead on the Settle & Carlisle line, which opened in 1876. Its superb setting is apparent here, as the 24 arches carry the streamlined A4 'Sir Nigel Gresley' more than 100 feet above the river valley.

▲ Knaresborough, in Yorkshire, is famous for its castle, high above the river Nidd, but the most frequently seen view of the town and river is this one, showing the viaduct. Completed in 1851, its four tall arches in decorative stone dominate both the town and the riverside. The architect, Thomas Grainger, took pains to make it blend with its surroundings. During its construction the viaduct collapsed and had to be rebuilt, delaying the opening of the line for three years. Such events, usually caused by poor workmanship, were not uncommon.

25876.

Lockwood Viaduct. Huddersfield.

◀ The Pennine landscape of Yorkshire made many demands upon the railway builders, and tunnels and viaducts abound. The best viaduct is probably Sir John Hawkshaw's Lockwood viaduct near Huddersfield, whose 32 arches were completed in 1850. This old postcard view shows how the narrowness of the arches seems to increase the sense of height (actually 122 feet at the highest point).

51

Southern England

CHELTENHAM TO ANDOVER

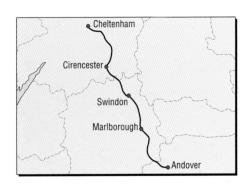

By the 1880s the railway map of Britain was quite comprehensive. Most of the main lines were in place and the tentacles of the network had spread into many corners of the country. However, railway building never ceased, despite the economic unpredictabiliy of the late Victorian era. The 1880s saw the construction of many branch and local connecting lines, to encourage freight traffic, feeder services to main lines and holiday business to the expanding coastal and inland resorts. Few new railways made great profits, but there always seemed to be plenty of investors and speculators prepared to put their money into railway projects, particularly when such projects seemed to fill a gap on the map. Several fairly substantial new railways were planned at this time, cross-country lines that seemed to offer more direct routes between major centres of conurbation and industry than already existed. A primary example was the line from Cheltenham to Andover, a long, rural north-to-south route whose strengths appeared to be its connections, Cheltenham, Andoversford, Swindon, Grafton and Andover with important

▲ Cheltenham's classic elegance has long been popular, as this Edwardian card indicates. The first railway arrived in 1840, with a grand, country house-like station called Lansdown. Other stations followed – Malvern Road and St James, for the GWR, and High Street, opened by the Midland in 1862.

London and South Western Ry. 787

From WATERLOO TO

Dowdeswell

Via Andover Junction.

► On a warm autumn afternoon in 1955 the Cheltenham to Southampton train arrives at Andoversford Junction, hauled by an old GWR Mogul, ready for the long cross-country route south.

◀ A quiet life and limited traffic made the M&SWJR an old-fashioned operation, even in the days of British Railways. This museum-like photograph shows the interior of the signal box at Andoversford Junction in 1961, when it was very near the end of its life. This is the box shown in the photograph below.

▲ This classic lost railway scene is Withington station, to the south of Andoversford, in 2005. Platforms and overbridge still stand as relics of the railway age, but they are now as mysterious as the structures of long-forgotten civilizations in the jungles of South America. It is hard to believe that trains stopped here less than 50 years ago. The real legacy of the closure programme of the 1960s is secret places like this, all over Britain.

◄ In a typical landscape of woods and gentle hills, an Andover to Cheltenham train crosses a small bridge near Withington, south of Andoversford, in the summer of 1961. The setting, the unhurried atmosphere and the elderly Southern Railway locomotive all capture the flavour of the country railway in its dying years. Within a few months the line had closed and all this had been consigned to history.

east–west routes, and thus its possibilities as a connecting line between the south and the Midlands. It was built from the early 1880s by two separate companies, the Swindon & Cheltenham Extension Railway and the Swindon, Marlborough & Andover Railway. Construction took some time and the line was not completed until 1891, by which time the two companies had merged to form themselves into the grandly named Midland & South Western Junction Railway. The aim was to run trains beyond Andover to Southampton via existing lines, but this was not achieved until 1894. The great hopes that had inspired the railway were never fulfilled, partly because the route itself was too rural and remote to generate much internal traffic and partly because the anticipated heavy through traffic from Southampton and the South to the Midlands never materialized. The railway went bankrupt in the 1890s, recovered and then managed to operate successfully until 1923, when it was absorbed into the GWR. Its salvation was military traffic, as the southern section served several bases, depots, camps and training areas, and the line was heavily used during both World Wars. By the late 1950s there was little traffic, and the route was a natural candidate for closure. It disappeared in 1961, along with many of its connecting lines. In the process Cirencester and Marlborough lost their mainline railway links. All that survived was the section north of Andover to the military stores depot at Ludgershall, and this is still used.

THE ROUTE TODAY

Although it took a long time to build, the Midland & South Western Junction was not a heavily engineered line. Its route is primarily through an open landscape of farmland and rolling hills, crossed by river valleys, notably the head waters of the Coln, Kennet and Thames. Today the open landscape makes it possible to trace much of the route, although it is not always accessible. Andoversford, the site of the junction with lines

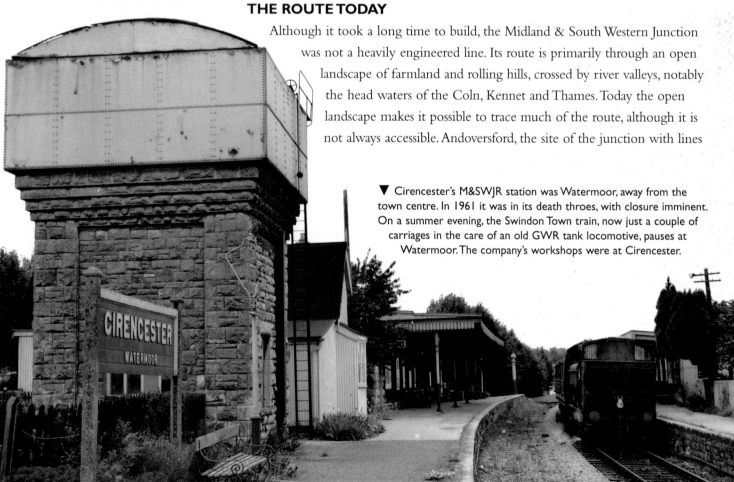

▼ Cirencester's M&SWJR station was Watermoor, away from the town centre. In 1961 it was in its death throes, with closure imminent. On a summer evening, the Swindon Town train, now just a couple of carriages in the care of an old GWR tank locomotive, pauses at Watermoor. The company's workshops were at Cirencester.

▲ The M&SWJR built Swindon Town station to the south of the huge GWR workshop complex and its busy London to Bristol route. This photograph was taken in the early 20th century, when the line was still reasonably busy.

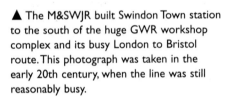

▲ Railway life has returned to a small part of the route, in the form of the Swindon & Cricklade Railway, a GWR-style preserved line. This is Blunsdon station, the railway's headquarters and depot.

to Banbury and Oxford, is worth exploring. Part of Cirencester's old Town station survives, but this was on the other line, the branch from Kemble, opened in the 1840s. To the south, the remains of a viaduct can be seen near South Cerney. Near Blunsdon, between Cricklade and Swindon, a short section has been re-opened as a preserved line by the Swindon & Cricklade Railway. From the outskirts of Swindon cyclists and walkers can follow the old trackbed through the village of Chiseldon and then through open countryside all the way to Marlborough. A bridlepath runs parallel for much of the way.

There is plenty to be seen between Marlborough and Grafton Junction as the route runs west of Savernake Forest and close to the Kennet & Avon Canal, but the story is complicated here. A branch to Marlborough was opened in 1864 and was initially incorporated into the M&SWJR's route. Traffic congestion resulted, so in 1896 the M&SWJ built a bypass called the Marlborough & Grafton Railway. Both then remained in service until 1933, when the original line was closed. South of Grafton the railway ran through an open landscape of gentle, bare hills, and nearly all the route to Andover survives, on low embankments or cut into the slopes of the hillside. Few structures remain, apart from small accommodation bridges. This has long been, and still is, military territory, with the army supplying plenty of traffic during the first half of the 20th century. A branch served the base at Tidworth, and the line between Ludgershall and Andover is still open for army use.

▲ While it never had particular tourist appeal, Andover did its best in the Edwardian period to put itself on the map. According to this card posted in 1911, the station was one of the town's highlights. There were actually two stations, the main Junction one, on the LSWR's main line west and the terminus of the M&SWJR's line, and Town station, which despite its name was well to the south on a connecting line to Stockbridge and Romsey along the Test valley.

▼ In a complicated coming together of lines at Wolfhall and Grafton Junctions, the M&SWJR met and crossed the GWR's main line west from Reading and its branch to Marlborough. In 1957, in a landscape setting typical of the route as a whole, a southbound train pauses at Wolfhall Junction.

6373

SOUTHERN RAILWAY.
(6/24)
TO
Stock 787
ANDOVER JUNCTION

MILITARY

RAILWAYS WERE first used by the army and the navy in the Victorian era, at arsenals, ordnance depots and dockyards. Since then, many military depots and sites have had their own railway system, linked to the national network.

By the 1890s military railway operations were controlled by the Royal Engineers, but the start of World War I saw the development of specialist units responsible for construction, operations and training. From 1905 the main training centre, covering all aspects of railway operation, was at Longmoor, in Hampshire; this remained in use until 1969.

During World War II many dockyards, army camps and airfields were rail connected, for the transport of personnel, equipment and supplies. Railways played a vital role throughout the war; preparations for the North African campaign, for example, involved 440 troop and 1,150 freight trains.

▲ Set up in 1905, the Longmoor Military Railway was a vast organization responsible for training generations of soldiers in all aspects of railway construction and operation. Connecting Liss and Bordon (seen above in 1934), the network had 11 stations and an entire railway infrastructure.

▼ World War I involved the railways on a massive scale. The Royal Engineers operated railways in many parts of the world. Training was usually undertaken at Longmoor. It is likely that this group, posing in front of an LSWR locomotive, have just finished their training.

▼ During the build-up to D-Day in 1944, railways were the prime movers of men and equipment, first to the concentration points and then southwards to the invasion ports. In April and May of that year over 24,000 special trains moved troops, ammunition and equipment, from tanks to bandages. Much of this was for the Americans, and during this time US Army Transport Corps locomotives ran on Britain's railways.

▲ From 1916, when conscription was introduced, women increasingly took over jobs hitherto done by men, many on the railways. In 1917 a group of women at London's Liverpool Street station display the uniforms of the various branches of the Great Eastern Railway.

AMBULANCE

N 1842 THE BRITISH government decreed that the railways would be required to carry troops as needed, and through the Victorian period trains became the primary carriers of troops and equipment, usually to embarkation ports. During World War I Southampton and other south coast ports were heavily used for shipping men and supplies to France and, for the first time, for receiving large numbers of wounded directly from battlefield dressing stations and field hospitals. There was, as a result, a huge demand for ambulance trains, in both France and Britain, and many carriages were converted for this purpose. Ambulance trains ran regular services carrying the wounded directly to military and civilian hospitals, using local stations. In addition some major hospitals, such as Netley and Lord Mayor Treloar, both in Hampshire, were served by special branch lines. In World War II, the burden on the railways was even greater, particularly after the Dunkirk evacuation and during the build-up to the D-Day invasion, and once again there was a massive requirement for ambulance trains.

▶ Ambulance trains required extensive paperwork. Typical is this World War I label from a Royal Artillery soldier's kitbag. He recovered from his wounds, and wrote on the back: 'Keep this souvenir!'

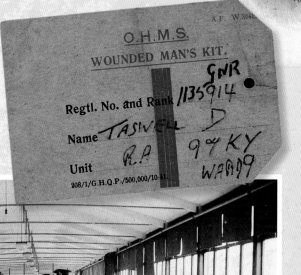

O.H.M.S.
WOUNDED MAN'S KIT.

Regtl. No. and Rank GNR 1135914
Name TASWELL D
Unit R.A. 9⁴ KY WARD9

A.F. W.3042

208/1/G.H.Q.P./500,000/10-41.

"ON SERVICE"

▲ Many women served as nurses and medical auxiliaries during World War I, both in field hospitals near the battlefields and in the huge hospital complexes built in Britain to handle the hundreds of thousands of casualties. Popular postcard images such as this one helped to maintain the glamorous vision that these women represented in the imagination of the ordinary soldier.

◀ Many postcards were issued during World War I showing wounded men in their hospital wards recovering from their injuries and often, as in this case, accompanied by the nurses who looked after them. They would all have been transported by ambulance trains.

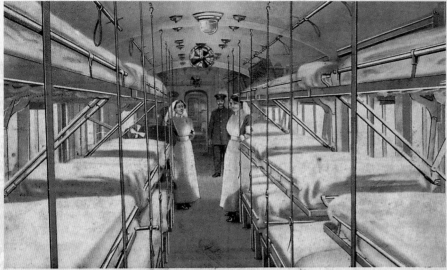

Interior of one of the Ward Cars of the Ambulance Train, constructed by the Caledonian Railway Company, on the order of the War Office, for conveyance of Wounded British Soldiers in France from the Front to the Sea-board.

◀ Large quantities of locomotives and rolling stock were sent from Britain to be used in France during World War I. Among these were ambulance trains built by many British railway companies to transport casualties from field hospitals to the coastal ports. This postcard shows a typical ward car, built by the Caledonian Railway.

▼ This World War I period postcard shows an ambulance train on the GWR network, used to transport casualties from south coast ports to hospitals in Wales and western England.

▼ Lord Mayor Treloar Hospital was a large military complex near Alton, in Hampshire, with its own stop on the old Basingstoke branch. This enabled casualties to be brought to the hospital direct from the quayside in Southampton. This photograph shows the hospital's platform after the line's closure.

ALTON TO WINCHESTER AND FAREHAM

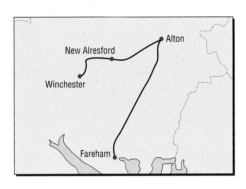

▼ The Alton to Winchester route was often used as a diversionary line, as here in May 1966, when the Waterloo to Bournemouth service, sent via Alton, is captured entering Medstead & Four Marks station, headed by the West Country class locomotive 'Salisbury', then very near the end of its life.

The London & South Western was a powerful and ambitious company, determined to retain control of railway services in what it regarded as its rightful territory, a large area of southern and south-western England. Its rival was the GWR, whose extensive network dominated Somerset, Devon and Cornwall. Through the latter part of the 19th century, the LSWR steadily pushed its lines westwards into the GWR heartland, ultimately reaching Ilfracombe, Bude and Padstow. In return, the GWR continually threatened to attack Southampton and Portsmouth, key LSWR strongholds. In the event, the GWR never penetrated beyond Winchester and Salisbury, but the threat was enough to encourage the LSWR to build lines that might otherwise have fallen to its arch rival. A typical example was the Alton, Alresford & Winchester Railway, a nominally independent company set up in 1861 to extend the already extant LSWR Alton branch. By the time the 17-mile line opened in 1865, the company had changed its name to the Mid Hants (Alton Lines) Railway, and within a few years the LSWR was in control.

► The Meon Valley line, running south from Alton to Fareham, remains largely visible, thanks to the undulating landscape. Sections have vanished, as ever, and much of the northern part of the route is private and inaccessible. However, surviving stations can sometimes be seen. Southwards from West Meon the trackbed is an official path, which makes a delightful walk along the valley. This is the view of the river Meon from an overbridge at Soberton.

London and South Western Ry. 787
From WATERLOO TO
ITCHEN ABBAS

Initially a quiet line offering an alternative route to Winchester, the railway came into its own during both World Wars as it offered a more direct route from Aldershot to Portsmouth and Southampton. It was heavily used by trains carrying troops and supplies and, because it was notorious for its steep grading, with a section known popularly as the Alps, double-heading was commonplace. After World War II it returned to a more rural existence, and lingered on under British Railways until closure in 1973, at which point Alton became once more the end of a branch line.

Although it seemed to have plenty of routes to the ports, the LSWR decided to create another one at the very end of the 19th century. This was to branch south from Alton and follow the Meon valley to a junction on the main Portsmouth line north of Fareham. This was opened on 1 June 1903, and from that point there were some through trains from Waterloo, labelled 'Gosport via the Meon Valley'. Although

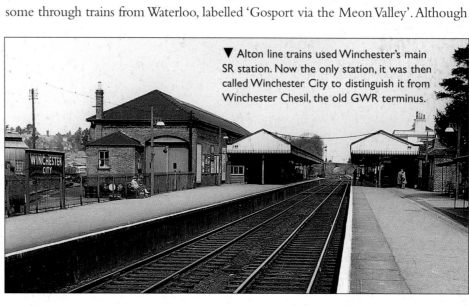

▼ Alton line trains used Winchester's main SR station. Now the only station, it was then called Winchester City to distinguish it from Winchester Chesil, the old GWR terminus.

▲ After the closure of the Meon Valley line, things remained in place for some time, quietly decaying. This 1957 view shows West Meon station and signal box with nature taking over. Today almost everything has gone and the site is much more heavily enclosed by trees.

▲ The hilly country of the Meon valley demanded relatively heavy engineering, with plenty of cuttings and embankments. These generally survive, making it quite easy to follow the route from adjacent minor roads. Typical is this view of the overgrown embankment on a private stretch between Privett and West Meon.

built to double-track standard, it was always a single-tracked route. It was a true country railway, passing through a delightfully varied landscape and following for much of its route the famous trout stream that gave it its name. Its most famous feature was its five stations, all built in the then fashionable Arts & Crafts style, with handsome stone mullions, curving gables and a lovely sense of proportion that showed the influence of architects such as Charles Voysey and Edwin Lutyens. Never busy, the line closed early, in 1955, and several of the stations have long ago been turned into delightful houses, which is exactly what they looked like in the first place. The most important moment in the line's uneventful history was in June 1944, when Winston Churchill and General Eisenhower, making final preparations for the D-Day invasion, stayed for a few days in a special train hidden by trees in a siding at Droxford station.

THE ROUTES TODAY

Ten years after closure of the Alton to Winchester route, the Mid-Hants Railway began its progressive re-opening of the line as a preserved steam railway. Today the Watercress Line, as it is called, is one of the premier lines in southern England, offering Southern Railway-style services between Alton and New Alresford. West of New Alresford the line is traceable and accessible in places, but full restoration as far as Winchester seems unlikely.

By contrast the Meon Valley line, since its closure, has suffered the fate of most abandoned railways. Much of the route is traceable, and it is easily followed by road. Some sections have been obliterated by farming and others are inaccessible, either overgrown or on private land.

▶ On a spring day in 1962 a train headed by an old Southern Railway U class locomotive pauses at Wickham station, the first stop on the Meon Valley line going north. At this point the line was closed as a through route, so this may have been a special or a railtour, even though there are very few passengers.

London and South Western Ry. 787
—
FROM WATERLOO TO
WEST MEON

66

As ever, there are tempting views from overbridges of lost trackbed and glimpses of now hidden stations. In places, the landscape is dramatic, with the line raised on high embankments, now wooded and carpeted with wild flowers. From West Meon south to Wickham the trackbed has been designated an official path, popular with local walkers, cyclists and horseriders. One of the best old railway footpaths in southern England, it follows the river closely for much of the way, at one point running across its watermeadows.

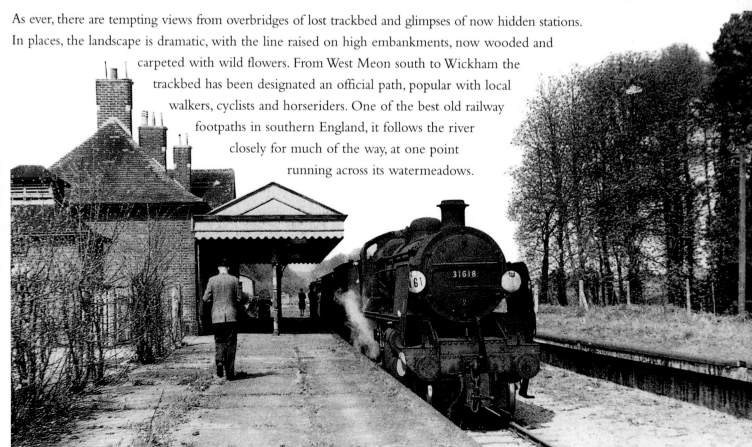

PAPER

IN 1906 A NETWORK of narrow-gauge railways was opened to service paper mills north of Sittingbourne, in Kent, an area chosen because of the easy access from docks, initially at Milton Creek but later and much more substantially at Ridham on the River Swale. With standard-gauge connections at each end, the network was busy through much of the 20th century, carrying workmen, raw materials (including china clay from Cornwall) and finished paper products. For the workforce, the railway also operated scheduled services.

From Sittingbourne the line is carried for half a mile through Milton Regis on a raised viaduct, one of the first structures in Britain built from reinforced concrete. At its peak in the 1950s, it was an extensive network with a number of stations, including Milton Regis, Kemsley Down and Ridham Dock; up to a dozen steam locomotives could be seen in use at any one time, many with distinctive spark-arresting chimneys, fitted to reduce the risk of fire when operating within the paper mills. Regular use of the railway ended in 1969, but Bowater Paper Company kept a section intact after closure. As a result, two miles of the network survive as a preserved line called the Sittingbourne & Kemsley Light Railway, a rare example of an industrial line in preservation. The railway has a large collection of 2ft 6in gauge locomotives, including two that were used on the line when it first opened. Its carriages are from the former military Chattenden & Upnor Railway, a line on the Isle of Grain, north of Chatham, built by the Royal Engineers and subsequently taken over by the Admiralty.

▲ The railway was still busy in the 1960s. Here two Bowater locomotives are on shunting duties. Various types of rolling stock can be seen on the extensive network visible in the background.

◄ Another Bowater locomotive, 'Melior', shunts wagons at Sittingbourne in 1959, against a backdrop of bales of different types of paper. Some are newsprint, one of the important products of the mill.

In 1966 the railway was nearing the end of its life, as reflected by the ancient rolling stock being shunted here at Ridham Dock. Against a backdrop of wastepaper bales, this view of 'Superb' – a locomotive that has survived into preservation – clearly shows the spark-arrester on the chimney.

Ever wary of the dangers of fire, Bowater also used Barclay fireless locomotives, as seen here in 1966. Designed to be powered by high-pressure steam drawn from a fixed supply, and regularly recharged, these locomotives were used in many industrial and military settings where fires and explosions were a risk.

HASTINGS TO ASHFORD

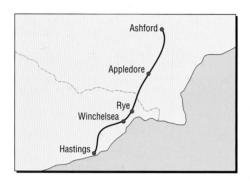

In 1851 the South Eastern Railway, a company gradually expanding its network in east Kent, opened a line from Hastings to Ashford. For the South Eastern it was a logical connecting line, but for the residents of a remote part of Kent on the edge of the Romney Marshes, it was a revolution. Sleepy little towns such as Rye and Winchelsea, still stuck in the 18th century amid the mystique of the Cinque Ports, were suddenly part of the modern world. Rye was the main beneficiary, gaining a modernized harbour, a grand classical station in the Italianate style (William Tress at his best) and, ultimately, its own local railway network. Winchelsea was not so lucky as the railway kept well to the north of the town. Other stops along the route were at that time little more than wayside halts, serving tiny communities. In due course a branch was opened from Appledore to New Romney, Lydd and Dungeness, which traversed the flat marshland and made accessible southern England's most unusual and remote landscape. By this time Hastings was discovering a new life as a holiday centre and the old village of Ashford was turning itself into a thriving and rapidly expanding railway town to service the works established there in the 1840s. From this point not much changed. The South Eastern joined its rivals, subsequently becoming the Southern Railway and in the end part of the Southern Region of British Railways. The New Romney branch, which from the 1920s offered

▲ 'Having a Good Time at Hastings' is the title of this photograph of a group of happy holidaymakers on the beach. It was taken in the 1930s, when Hastings was at its peak as a fashionable resort, thanks largely to the railway and its smart, modernist publicity.

▶ East of Hastings the line crosses the flat landscape that borders the Romney Marshes, framed to the north by a line of hills. Rye, set on a hill and topped by its church tower, is a distinctive and dominant feature, seen easily from an approaching train.

▲ In 1966 the railway was nearing the end of its life, as reflected by the ancient rolling stock being shunted here at Ridham Dock. Against a backdrop of wastepaper bales, this view of 'Superb' – a locomotive that has survived into preservation – clearly shows the spark-arrester on the chimney.

◄ Ever wary of the dangers of fire, Bowater also used Barclay fireless locomotives, as seen here in 1966. Designed to be powered by high-pressure steam drawn from a fixed supply, and regularly recharged, these locomotives were used in many industrial and military settings where fires and explosions were a risk.

HASTINGS TO ASHFORD

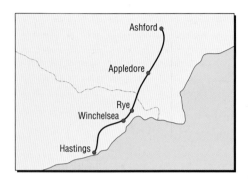

In 1851 the South Eastern Railway, a company gradually expanding its network in east Kent, opened a line from Hastings to Ashford. For the South Eastern it was a logical connecting line, but for the residents of a remote part of Kent on the edge of the Romney Marshes, it was a revolution. Sleepy little towns such as Rye and Winchelsea, still stuck in the 18th century amid the mystique of the Cinque Ports, were suddenly part of the modern world. Rye was the main beneficiary, gaining a modernized harbour, a grand classical station in the Italianate style (William Tress at his best) and, ultimately, its own local railway network. Winchelsea was not so lucky as the railway kept well to the north of the town. Other stops along the route were at that time little more than wayside halts, serving tiny communities. In due course a branch was opened from Appledore to New Romney, Lydd and Dungeness, which traversed the flat marshland and made accessible southern England's most unusual and remote landscape. By this time Hastings was discovering a new life as a holiday centre and the old village of Ashford was turning itself into a thriving and rapidly expanding railway town to service the works established there in the 1840s. From this point not much changed. The South Eastern joined its rivals, subsequently becoming the Southern Railway and in the end part of the Southern Region of British Railways. The New Romney branch, which from the 1920s offered

▲ 'Having a Good Time at Hastings' is the title of this photograph of a group of happy holidaymakers on the beach. It was taken in the 1930s, when Hastings was at its peak as a fashionable resort, thanks largely to the railway and its smart, modernist publicity.

► East of Hastings the line crosses the flat landscape that borders the Romney Marshes, framed to the north by a line of hills. Rye, set on a hill and topped by its church tower, is a distinctive and dominant feature, seen easily from an approaching train.

◄ There have been several stations at Hastings. This early 20th-century postcard shows it during the era of the South Eastern & Chatham Railway, a smart and efficient company whose network covered much of Kent. The station then served many routes, to the west, the east and the north, and London expresses would stand next to locals for Ashford.

HASTINGS STATION-DEPARTURE PLATFORM.
SOUTH EASTERN & CHATHAM RY.

► Although ignored by the railway, Winchelsea was a picturesque town rich in history and popular with visitors. As a result it generated plenty of postcards, which often blended rural romanticism with history. This card depicts Strand Gate, a legacy of the town's time as a busy port in the Middle Ages.

The Strand Gate, Winchelsea

From a Water Colour Drawing by W. H. Borrow.

Rye and Camber Tram.

▲ Rye had two railways of its own, apart from t
One was a short branch to the harbour, but mor
was the Rye & Camber Railway, opened initially t
Club in 1895 and extended to Camber Sands in
a very basic operation, with primitive locomotive
of ancient carriages, but its eccentricity added so
town. It was closed in 1939.

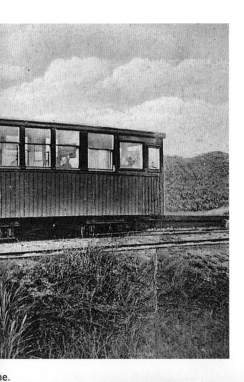

a connection with the Romney, Hythe & Dymchurch Railway, was closed to passengers in the 1960s, although part of the route remains open for trains serving the nuclear power station at Dungeness. Promoted as the smallest public railway in the world and deservedly famous, the Romney, Hythe & Dymchurch lives on in splendid isolation.

THE JOURNEY

Since privatization of the railways, the route between Hastings and Ashford has seen the comings and goings of a number of operators, along with their liveries. However, even in standard modern stock the journey is still a pleasure and offers, as it always has, a vision of a remote and little-known region of England. It is a true country railway, a kind of time warp between slices of the modern world. At one end is Hastings, a town built on history and a resort that has known better days. It is now graced with a new station, built to replace the former Art Deco palace that was a sad memorial of the town's great days in the 1930s. At the other end of the line is Ashford, with its glittering new international station, the gateway to Europe, surrounded by the clutter of the former railway works that were the birthplace of some of the most famous railway locomotives that ever ran on the railways of southern England.

◀ The windmill on the river bank near the station has always been a distinctive Rye landmark. This 2003 photograph shows somewhat ancient class 205 diesel-electric stock.

PARIS
BY
GOLDEN ARROW

FRANCE & BELGIUM

IN 1848 THE LSWR began to operate shipping services to the Channel Islands and Le Havre, in France, the start of a connection between boats and trains that continued until the break-up of British Railways in 1984. By the 1860s railway companies were running ships from ports all over Britain, but the emphasis was on services across the English Channel, and notably the short sea routes. In 1853 the South Eastern Railway started a Folkestone to Boulogne service; many others followed, using ports as diverse as Southampton, Portsmouth, Dover, Ramsgate, Sheerness, Port Victoria on the Isle of Grain and Harwich. The emphasis was on passengers but freight services were also run. Competition was rife and companies fought for passengers by offering the fastest and most comfortable ships, with the timings often based on the total journey, for example London to Paris or Brussels, rather than just the Channel crossing. These depended upon joint operations with French or Belgian railways, many of which continued until 1984. By this standard, the most successful routes were Dover to Calais and Ostend, and Newhaven to Dieppe. With short crossings, the ships were designed primarily as fast day boats, catering initially for train passengers but increasingly for road vehicles as well. From 1947 all routes came under the control of British Railways, and from 1970 all were marketed under the Sealink brand.

ENGLAND–BELGIUM

sleep

your

way

in comfort

by BRITISH RAILWAYS

via Harwich via Dover

28th MAY to 30th SEPTEMBER 1961

BRITISH RAILWAYS s.s. "DINARD" 1998

▲ On some of the longer crossings there were both day and night services and ships were accordingly equipped with cabins. As this 1961 leaflet indicates, the slower overnight services were promoted on the basis of comfort and relaxation.

◀ Cross-channel ferries were often technically advanced in terms of design, fittings, speed, reliability and handling, and were marketed as such. This 1950s postcard shows the passenger ferry *Dinard* leaving Dover for Calais.

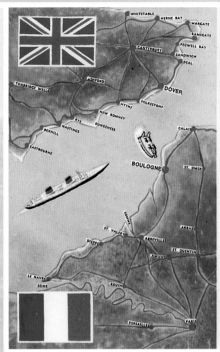

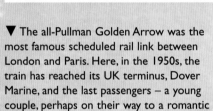

SEASPEED HOVERCRAFT
DOVER — BOULOGNE

◀ In order to offer a faster service for passengers and vehicles, British Railways began to operate cross-channel hovercraft services in 1966 on short routes. From 1970 these were marketed under the Seaspeed name.

GO RAIL-AIR TO

SUMMER 1964

PARiS

UNDER 4¼ HOURS
CITY CENTRE TO CITY CENTRE

FROM £9. 18. 0.
RETURN

TOURIST CLASS AIR TRAVEL

▼ The all-Pullman Golden Arrow was the most famous scheduled rail link between London and Paris. Here, in the 1950s, the train has reached its UK terminus, Dover Marine, and the last passengers – a young couple, perhaps on their way to a romantic weekend – stroll towards the ferry.

▶ The opening of the Channel Tunnel in 1994 simplified travel to Europe. Until then, speed was the essence and British Railways did its best to compete with air travel. In the 1960s the Silver Arrow service seemed to offer the best of both worlds: rail travel direct to and from the airports, with a short hop between.

22 March — 24 October 1964

SILVER ARROW

FLECHE D'ARGENT London (Victoria Station) · London (Gatwick) · Le Touquet · Paris (Gare du Nord)

Silver Arrow Service · British United Airways · Portland House · Stag Place · London S.W.1.
Telephone Tate Gallery 9066

RAIL CENTRE: LEWES

SET IN A COMMANDING position above the wide valley of the Ouse, Lewes has been a town of distinction since the Norman period. Medieval streets, Georgian architecture and its considerable wealth and industry, derived from its role as the county town of Sussex, aroused the attention of early railway builders. Lines linking the town to London and Brighton were opened in the late 1840s, the first by the London & Brighton Railway (later the giant London, Brighton & South Coast Railway), and the second by the Brighton, Lewes & Hastings Railway, soon to be part of the LB&SCR. The branch to Newhaven was built at the same time, to allow the LB&SCR to develop the harbour and operate services to France. A decade later the Lewes & Uckfield line opened a through route to Tunbridge Wells. The final arrival, in 1882, was the line north to East Grinstead, which was also the first to close, in 1958. With lines converging from six directions,

EAST GRINSTEAD
An old market town, East Grinstead expanded rapidly in the 19th century after the arrival of the railway. The mixture of 18th-century and early and late Victorian architecture shown in this 1905 card of London Road underlines this. The message is to the point: 'I Hope you liked the cake I sent.' By 1905 the town was connected by rail to London, Brighton, Three Bridges and Tunbridge Wells. Part of the Brighton route is now the Bluebell Railway.

Lewes became a busy place, at one time boasting three stations. The one in use today, set below the town and approached by steep curves and a long tunnel from the north, dates from 1889 and is rich in period detail.

BRIGHTON
The Brighton Pavilion ceased to be a royal palace early in the 19th century but, as this card indicates, it retained its popularity among visitors through the Victorian and Edwardian eras. Brighton's position as a premier south coast resort soon attracted the interest of railway builders, and the line to London opened in 1841. Other lines followed, making the town the centre of a considerable south coast network and an important jewel in the crown of the London, Brighton & South Coast Railway. By the end of the century the journey time to London had been reduced to about an hour, greatly encouraging commuting to the capital.

TUNBRIDGE WELLS

A famous spa and resort with a long history, Tunbridge Wells was little affected by the coming of the railway in 1846 and today its heart has retained a pre-Victorian atmosphere. At that point it was at the western limits of the South Eastern's network. Later, in the 1860s, the LB&SCR's line from Lewes via Uckfield arrived. On its way, this passed through Eridge, whose rather elaborate but largely 19th-century castle was the seat of the Marquess of Abergavenny. Presumably he is the rather fierce gentleman depicted in this Edwardian card, determined to put his castle on the tourist map despite its cluttered Victorian gothic appearance, which at that time would have seemed completely at odds with the classical elegance of Tunbridge Wells.

Lewes station in 1934

LEWES

NEWHAVEN

Newhaven was a sleepy fishing harbour when the LB&SCR's branch from Lewes arrived in 1847. Quickly revitalized and hugely expanded, the port soon fulfilled that company's ambitions to became an important operator of ferries to France. From the 1860s through to the 1920s Newhaven to Dieppe was the premier cross-channel route, offering the quickest London to Paris journey.

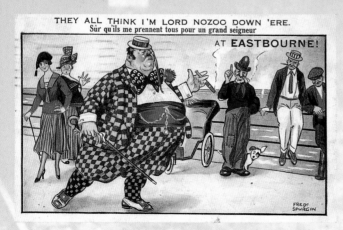

EASTBOURNE

When modern Eastbourne was created by the 7th Duke of Devonshire in 1834 from an insignificant little village, his plan was to build an elegant resort for people who wanted something more refined than the raffish gaiety and vulgarity of its neighbour, Brighton. Initially the town was all parks and gardens, tree-lined roads, smart terraces and hotels, with hardly a shop to be seen. Some of this early quality survives, but the railway, which first reached the town in 1846, inevitably brought changes – and a different kind of clientele, as this early 1920s postcard by Fred Spurgin suggests. The present, rather eccentric French-style station dates from 1886 and reflects the extravagant taste of the LB&SCR.

IRELAND & THE CHANNEL ISLANDS

WHEN IRELAND joined the United Kingdom in 1800, communications became of paramount importance. The transport of mail inspired firstly Telford's road to Holyhead and then the building of rail links from London. Existing ferry services were expanded and, as more railway companies became interested in the Irish trade, so other ferry routes opened, many initiated or owned by those railways. For example, the GWR developed routes from Fishguard, the Glasgow & South Western involved itself in the development of Stranraer, and the Midland promoted Heysham. However, the principal route was Holyhead to Kingstown, Dublin, started by the Chester & Holyhead Railway in 1848. By the end of the 19th century there were large numbers of railway-owned ships and ferries, many with a reputation for being fast, modern and comfortable vessels. This pattern continued through the 20th century, with all the ships becoming

S.S. ANGLIA
DIRECT SERVICE BETWEEN HOLYHEAD & DUBLIN.
THE MOST COMFORTABLE ROUTE BETWEEN LONDON & DUBLIN

▲ This card, issued in the Edwardian era by the LNWR, shows the SS *Anglia*, one of the fastest and most modern vessels on the Irish routes. Highly regarded, they were by modern standards small ships.

part of British Railways in 1948. They then operated under the Sealink name until privatization in 1984.

The London & South Western Railway was the first company to run ships to the Channel Islands, in the late 1840s. Others followed but this route was always dominated by competition between the LSWR and, later, Southern Railway ships from Southampton and the Great Western services from Weymouth. Freight was as important as passenger traffic, and particularly the shipment to the mainland of flowers, fruit and vegetables. Today rival routes still serve the Channel Isles, but all railway connections have gone.

BRITISH
RAILWAYS
SERVICES
& FARES
to and from
the
CHANNEL
ISLANDS

◄ British Railways produced this brochure in 1961 to promote their new ships on the Weymouth to the Channel Islands service. It offered 'New Standards of Comfort'.

Southern Railway.

STOCK. 787 DD.

(5/28)

From ____

TO

GUERNSEY

▲ In 1959 the Channel Islands boat train sets off from Weymouth quay through the town behind an old GWR tank engine. The boat left Jersey at 8am and docked at 3pm. The express would leave the main station at 4pm, reaching Waterloo at 7.35pm. Trains used the quay tramway until the late 1980s.

▶ This 1960s timetable shows the great range of Irish ferry services operated at that time by British Railways. Steamer services were a major part of the BR empire, on Irish, cross-Channel and North Sea routes, and even on Lake Windermere.

IRISH CROSS CHANNEL **TIMETABLES**

12th SEPTEMBER 1960 TO 11th JUNE 1961
OR UNTIL FURTHER NOTICE

HOLYHEAD STATION.
DEPARTURE OF THE UP BOAT EXPRESS.

◀ An Edwardian view of Holyhead station as the Up Boat Express prepares to depart. Issued by the LNWR, the image offers a somewhat 'upmarket' vision of travel on the primary, and thus crowded, route between Ireland and Britain.

East Anglia

CAMBRIDGE TO COLCHESTER

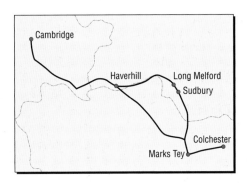

Today the train journey from Cambridge to Colchester is laborious, involving a long loop via Newmarket, Bury St Edmunds and Ipswich. Until the 1960s the journey was much simpler and more direct, and there was even a choice of routes. It all started in 1847, when the Colchester, Stour Valley, Sudbury & Halstead Railway was finally given authorization for its 35-mile line to Cambridge. Construction was slow, with sections opening independently, and the whole route was not completed until 1865. By this time another company, the Colne Valley & Halstead Railway, had opened a line that offered a parallel but more direct journey over part of the route, between Chappel and Haverhill. These two railways then enjoyed their independent but inter-related existence for some years. The first was absorbed into the Great Eastern in 1898, but the smaller Colne Valley line survived on its own until 1923, despite long periods of financial uncertainty. Both continued to operate through the LNER era and into the time of British Railways. However, as country routes serving rural regions they had a distinctly uncertain future. Closure came in the 1960s, along with the branch northwards from Long Melford to Bury St Edmunds.

CAMBRIDGE.—The Bridge of Sighs, St. John's College.

▲ Clare station, the only one in Britain built within the walls of a medieval castle, survives almost intact, as part of a country park. Buildings, a goods shed, both platforms and a crane are all to be enjoyed.

◄ Hundreds of postcards have tried for a century to capture the particular blend of romance and architecture that is the essence of Cambridge. This early example showing St John's College and the Bridge of Sighs over the Cam is typical.

▼ A large locomotive and a disproportionately small train made up of a couple of carriages form the lunchtime stopping train from Colchester to Cambridge in October 1959. This is Stoke station, to the east of Haverhill.

THE ROUTE TODAY

The section from Sudbury to Marks Tey, on the main London to Colchester line, was spared and this remains as a fully operating branch line, a rarity in the age of Network Rail and private operators. Short sections of the line from Haverhill to Chappel also survive as preserved railways, with the East Anglian Railway Museum in the old Chappel & Wakes Colne station, and the Colne Valley Railway operating steam trains along a mile or so near Castle Hedingham.

The former Colchester & Stour Valley line branched off from the Great Eastern's Cambridge to London line near Great Shelford and ran east to Haverhill through an open landscape. Traces remain, though not always accessible. At Haverhill, where the Halstead line branched away to the south, there were originally two stations, North and South, but South, on the Halstead line, and approached via a big brick viaduct that still stands, closed in 1924. Running for much of its length alongside the river Colne, the Halstead line was a pretty, rural route through a gentle landscape. It closed in 1962 and since then some sections have completely vanished, while others are hidden among fields and copses. The Stour Valley line, east from Haverhill alongside the river all the way to Bures, south of Sudbury, had a more active life. Some stretches are clearly visible from the adjacent road, while others have completely disappeared. Bridges have gone, notably the many river crossings, and much of the surviving trackbed is on private land. The surprise is Clare station, preserved as part of a country park, with a short section now used as a footpath. During World War II this station was kept busy by Stradishall, an RAF bomber base to the north. Cavendish and Long Melford are famously attractive towns, but little remains of their railway past. At Sudbury station, the real railway suddenly begins. The journey from here to Colchester, through a landscape filled with echoes of Constable, is delightful, giving a hint of what the rest must have been like.

▼ On a summer Saturday in 1956 the train from Cambridge to Marks Tey drifts slowly into Clare station. The antique locomotive, at the end of its working life, and the assortment of ill-matched carriages behind it are typical of the line at this time. With its colour-washed houses, pargetted plasterwork, Clare always had plenty of visitors, most of whom would have travelled by train.

▲ Parts of the old railway line from Haverhill to Sudbury via Halstead have vanished, while short sections have come back to life as preserved lines. In between are sections adopted by farmers as access tracks, such as this example, near Ridgewell.

► As an army town of long standing, Colchester was used to pomp and performance. The town's pageant was always popular. Here, in 1909, scenes relevant to the history of Colchester were acted out, in this case the arrival of the Roman Emperor Claudius and his retinue.

Colchester Pageant
Emperor Claudius and Retinue

BOAT TRAINS

▼ In 1956 the Cunarder comes to rest at Cunard's passenger reception area in Southampton docks, having run non-stop from Waterloo. The train included Pullmans and ample baggage cars.

RAILWAY COMPANIES began to operate trains to connect with shipping services in the 1840s, initially in Scotland and for cross-Channel sailings from Dover and Folkestone. However, the vaguaries of tides made it impossible to schedule regular services, a problem not fully overcome until the 1880s, when deep-water harbours were constructed. The first dedicated boat train in Britain to operate to a fixed timetable was the Irish Mail. By the early 20th century the boat train had become quite common, and many companies ran special services to Channel, Irish and North Sea ports, to Liverpool, to Fishguard and elsewhere. Some were given suitable names, such as the Hook Continental, the American Express or the Manxman. In many cases, special carriages were used, with Pullman-style comfort and full catering facilities. The boat train was probably at its peak in the 1920s and 1930s but some services survived until the 1980s, albeit in a comparatively basic form. Boat trains also ran to service specific trans-Atlantic liners, such as the *Queen Mary* at Southampton. Much rarer were train ferries, transporting railway vehicles across stretches of water. First used on the Forth and the Tay, these did not become common until World War 1. Freight was the prime user but from 1936 the Night Ferry carried sleeping cars between Dover and Dunkirk.

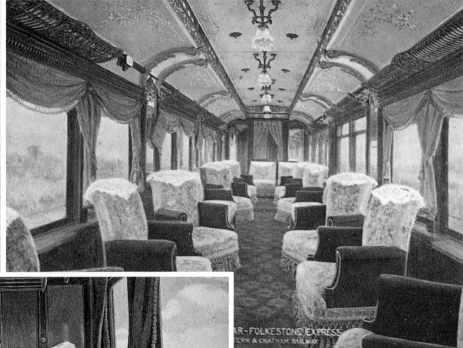

▲ Edwardian elegance in the drawing room car of the Folkestone Express, a regular boat train operated by the South Eastern & Chatham Railway from London Victoria.

AFTERNOON TEA IN THE SALON-DE-LUXE
L. & N.W. AMERICAN SPECIAL.

◀ This LNWR promotional postcard of about 1910 shows ladies enjoying afternoon tea in the Salon-de-Luxe on the American Express, a scheduled boat train service between London and Liverpool.

▲ Parts of the old railway line from Haverhill to Sudbury via Halstead have vanished, while short sections have come back to life as preserved lines. In between are sections adopted by farmers as access tracks, such as this example, near Ridgewell.

► As an army town of long standing, Colchester was used to pomp and performance. The town's pageant was always popular. Here, in 1909, scenes relevant to the history of Colchester were acted out, in this case the arrival of the Roman Emperor Claudius and his retinue.

Colchester Pageant
Emperor Claudius and Retinue

Boat Trains

RAILWAY COMPANIES began to operate trains to connect with shipping services in the 1840s, initially in Scotland and for cross-Channel sailings from Dover and Folkestone. However, the vaguaries of tides made it impossible to schedule regular services, a problem not fully overcome until the 1880s, when deep-water harbours were constructed. The first dedicated boat train in Britain to operate to a fixed timetable was the Irish Mail. By the early 20th century the boat train had become quite common, and many companies ran special services to Channel, Irish and North Sea ports, to Liverpool, to Fishguard and elsewhere. Some were given suitable names, such as the Hook Continental, the American Express or the Manxman. In many cases, special carriages were used, with Pullman-style comfort and full catering facilities. The boat train was probably at its peak in the 1920s and 1930s but some services survived until the 1980s, albeit in a comparatively basic form. Boat trains also ran to service specific trans-Atlantic liners, such as the *Queen Mary* at Southampton. Much rarer were train ferries, transporting railway vehicles across stretches of water. First used on the Forth and the Tay, these did not become common until World War 1. Freight was the prime user but from 1936 the Night Ferry carried sleeping cars between Dover and Dunkirk.

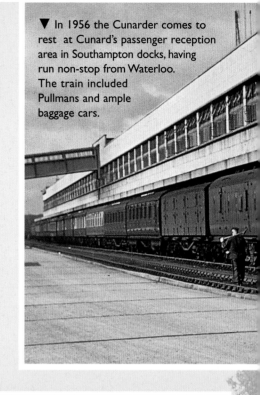

▼ In 1956 the Cunarder comes to rest at Cunard's passenger reception area in Southampton docks, having run non-stop from Waterloo. The train included Pullmans and ample baggage cars.

▲ Edwardian elegance in the drawing room car of the Folkestone Express, a regular boat train operated by the South Eastern & Chatham Railway from London Victoria.

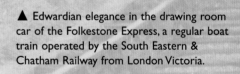

◄ This LNWR promotional postcard of about 1910 shows ladies enjoying afternoon tea in the Salon-de-Luxe on the American Express, a scheduled boat train service between London and Liverpool.

AFTERNOON TEA IN THE SALON-DE-LUXE
L. & N.W. AMERICAN SPECIAL.

▼ The traditional boat train was re-introduced in 1980 by the Venice Simplon Orient Express. Here, in 1991, the long rake of restored Pullman cars approaches Folkestone harbour.

▶ British Railways operated freight-only train ferries from Dover and Harwich, as this 1960s brochure indicates. Services continued until the opening of the Channel tunnel.

BRITISH RAILWAYS DAILY SERVICES VIA

DOVER-DUNKERQUE HARWICH-ZEEBRUGGE

British Rail | Shipping Services

RAIL CENTRE: CAMBRIDGE

TRAINS CAME QUITE EARLY to Cambridge, with the opening of the grand Romanesque-style, arcaded station in 1845. Its architect was probably Francis Thompson and its builder was the Eastern Counties Railway, later the Great Eastern, whose ambitions for the city were thwarted by the university colleges' determination to keep the railway as far away as possible. Today the station is still inconveniently placed, a mile from the centre. From the start it was an unusual station, both in the grandeur of its architecture and in its having only one long platform, used by trains in both directions thanks to cross-over facilities in the centre. Remarkably, both these features survive today and the latter, common in the 1840s and 1850s, is now very rare. As the station expanded into a significant rail centre, accommodating trains from several directions operated by four companies, the Great Eastern, the Midland, the Great Northern and the LNWR, the single platform became a logistical nightmare. Yet it survived. An attempt was made in the 1880s to create a new city centre station, but once again the colleges successfully resisted it. In its heyday, Cambridge offered two routes to London, via Hitchin and Bishop's Stortford and lines to Newmarket, Norwich, Bury St Edmunds, Colchester, Bedford, St Ives and Huntingdon, Ely and King's Lynn, March and beyond, and Fordham, with a connection for Mildenhall. There were also extensive goods sidings for the various

PETERBOROUGH

Peterborough's great cathedral, dating from the 11th to the 15th centuries, is the town's most famous sight and has been the subject of thousands of cards, including this 1950s example. In railway terms, Peterborough is a Great Northern city, and that company was responsible for much of its 19th-century development, railway and otherwise. Trains from Cambridge travelled via March, as they still do, but used Peterborough East station.

BEDFORD

Most of the scenes on this old card feature the river Great Ouse, and certainly the most attractive parts of Bedford are by the river. Also included is the statue of the town's most famous resident, John Bunyan, who lived here from 1655 until his death in 1688. Also shown is the County School, one of four public schools in Bedford. Plans for a railway to Cambridge were first drawn up in 1836. Ten years later the Bedford to Bletchley section was opened, but the line onwards to Cambridge took nearly another 20 years to complete. It was finally opened in 1862 by the Bedford & Cambridge Railway, which was then quickly absorbed by the LNWR. This route was closed in 1968.

operating companies. During World War II Cambridge was an important centre for traffic serving many of the East Anglian airfields and other military sites. Today many of the routes and connections have gone, notably the lines to Bedford, Colchester and Huntingdon, but Cambridge remains a remarkable busy station. In the 1980s it was extensively restored, so it is easy for passengers using the station today to imagine how it must have looked when it was new.

Ely Cathedral from the Ouse

ELY

Ely's cathedral rides like a ship above the surrounding landscape and, not surprisingly, it also dominates the city. The famous view is this one from the river Ouse, seen here on a card posted in 1921. The Eastern Counties Railway reached the city in 1845 and its classical station by Francis Thompson still exists, making the most of its riverside setting. Despite its remote location, Ely became a significant rail centre in its own right in the 19th century, the meeting point for six lines. Remarkably, five of these are still in operation. The sixth was a rural branch westwards, opened by the Ely, Haddenham & Sutton Railway in 1866 and extended ten years later to St Ives. Then known as the Ely & St Ives, and part of the GER by 1898, it closed in 1931.

London train leaving Cambridge in 1958

CAMBRIDGE

The River Lark, Mildenhall

MILDENHALL

Famous for the hoard of late Roman treasure discovered in 1946, Mildenhall has a long history, evidenced in its large church. In the 19th century the river Lark, seen here in 1915, was a navigation, and the town relied on it until the branch line arrived from Fordham. This included one of Britain's few dedicated golf club halts. Busy in World War II serving a nearby USAF base, the branch closed in the 1960s.

High Street and Jubilee Tower, Newmarket.

NEWMARKET

Posted in 1905, this card shows race horses being exercised along Newmarket's main street, overshadowed by the then quite new Queen Victoria Jubilee Tower. By this time, horses were regularly transported to and from the town by train, perhaps via the great baroque station of 1848. This sumptuous building, in its style and detail unlike any other in Britain, was demolished in the 1970s, after years of disuse following the opening of a new and smaller station in 1902. The baroque masterpiece was the creation of the Newmarket Railway, whose line initially to Great Chesterford and then to Cambridge was finally completed in 1851, with the help of the Eastern Counties Railway.

DOCKS AND SHIPYARDS

THE RAPID EXPANSION of ports and docks in early Victorian Britain at first disregarded the railway, and it was not until the 1850s that docks were built with direct rail access. By this time many railway companies had interests in docks and warehousing and were rapidly developing new port facilities in many places, including London, Plymouth, Fishguard, Barrow and Grangemouth, as well as on the Mersey, around Hull and in south Wales. In 1923 the GWR found itself to be the largest dock owner in the world. Some docks were specialized, such as the coal ports of south Wales and the north-east, or the fishing ports of the east coast and Scotland, but the most trade was generated by general ports, designed to handle cargoes of every kind and built with every sort of modern facility. The greatest of all the railway ports was Southampton, developed by the LSWR from 1892 into a port system capable of handling the largest ships and huge quantities of passengers and freight. In 1953 over 12 million tons passed through Southampton, which by then was run by British Railways.

▼ Modern docks with rail access were capable of handling every type of cargo, at a time when Britain was still a major exporter of manufactured goods. A typical cargo in 1924 was railway locomotives, built at the Vulcan Foundry for the Indian railways and here being loaded at Birkenhead docks.

◀ Immingham Deep Water Dock was developed by the Great Central Railway, an ambitious company keen to control the Humber region. This Edwardian promotional postcard gives a rather simplified view, but it does reflect the domination of the dock and its operations by the railway company.

▶ Many shipbuilders had extensive dockside railway systems in their yards for moving raw materials and finished components. For many activities, specialized handling was required: this group of locomotives equipped with cranes was photographed at William Doxford's Pallion Shipyard in Sunderland, where, in 1964, steam was still king.

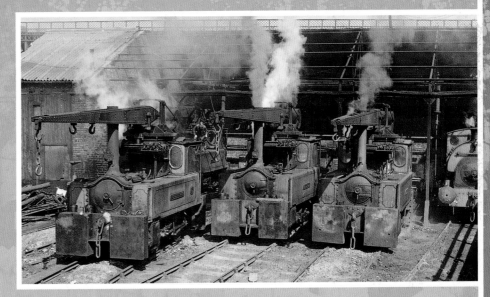

▼ In 1963 a diesel shunter moves a group of wagons along the quayside at Dover Eastern Docks, overlooked by Dover Castle on the horizon. At this point many docks in Britain were still primarily rail-operated. Today few quays ever see a train, though the tracks often remain, a derelict reminder of past glories.

IPSWICH to LOWESTOFT

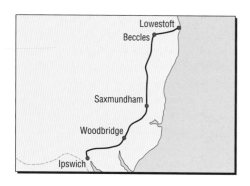

The rural journey from Ipswich to Lowestoft is that delightful anachronism, a proper country railway. It is also a real rarity: an alternative route of the kind weeded out so assiduously by Dr Beeching. The quickest way to Lowestoft is a dash up the old Great Eastern main line to Norwich and then a local train to the coast. More leisurely, and far more enjoyable, is the country route via Woodbridge and Beccles. It is an irony that when it was built its investors, notably the tycoon and entrepreneur Sir Samuel Morton Peto, were inspired by the idea of a quicker and more direct route to Lowestoft that would naturally encourage rapid development of that town and its port. As so often, the line was built in several stages by different companies, and the history is confusing.

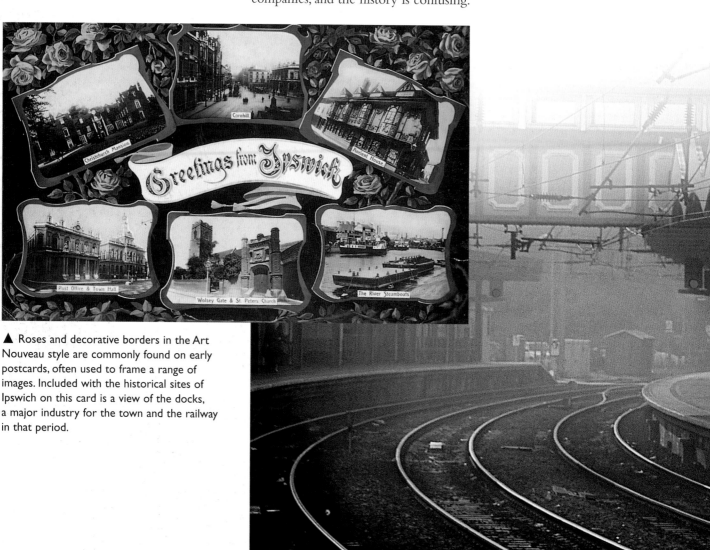

▲ Roses and decorative borders in the Art Nouveau style are commonly found on early postcards, often used to frame a range of images. Included with the historical sites of Ipswich on this card is a view of the docks, a major industry for the town and the railway in that period.

► There are two faces of Ipswich station, the mainline expresses to Norwich and London, and the little trains on cross-country routes. Typical of the latter is the single diesel railcar for Lowestoft, waiting to depart from platform 2 on a bright morning in 1994.

◄ Woodbridge is an attractive town set on the hillside above the tidal estuary of the Deben. The station overlooks the river and its boatyards. This view of the Crown Hotel hints at an earlier period in the town's history, before the railway arrived in the late 1850s.

▲ Saxmundham station is a typical east Suffolk station, square and classical in a simple manner. Today much of the route is single tracked and trains are rarely more than a couple of carriages. The long platform hints at greater things in the past, but this was always primarily a local line. Until the 1960s, passengers for Aldeburgh changed here.

First came the Halesworth, Beccles & Haddiscoe Railway, opened in 1854 to give inland towns access to Lowestoft and Norwich. Other small companies, the Yarmouth & Haddiscoe and the Lowestoft & Beccles, added bits and pieces. These and others were formed into the East Suffolk Railway from 1854, and it was this company that completed the line to Ipswich in 1859. A number of branches were also built, serving Framlingham, Snape and Aldeburgh. The line to Felixstowe, built by the Felixstowe Railway & Dock Company, came much later, in 1877, by which time the whole network had been merged into the Great Eastern Railway. The GER ran the East Suffolk line and its connections as a useful secondary route. Most traffic was, as a result, local and there were few through passenger services until after the 1920s, when holiday specials increased. Freight services were also mainly local, though the route was used by through milk and fish trains. Agriculture, local industry and the local harbours were the primary freight users.

Things stayed the same until the 1960s, by which time freight traffic had virtually ended. The branches were pruned, except for the flourishing Felixstowe line, which now served the giant container port. The Aldeburgh branch was also kept open to Leiston, for the nuclear power station at Sizewell. Today little has changed. The line is well used by local people, for school, work and play, and the single- or two-car trains are often full. The timetable is if anything better than it was in the 19th century.

THE JOURNEY

The journey is one of quiet pleasures: gentle East Anglian landscapes under big skies, with echoes of paintings by Cotman and Constable; pleasant river valleys with views of woodland and old farms; classic country towns, Woodbridge, Saxmundham, Halesworth, Beccles, many with great churches and the unchanged atmosphere of rural England. All are worth leaving the train for, even if the stations themselves are not always alluring. Halesworth was also the connecting point for the eccentric Southwold Railway, whose 9-mile narrow-gauge line followed the pretty valley of the Blyth. Set up in the 1870s, it offered four trains a day each way, and passengers travelled at 16 miles per hour in Continental-style carriages with verandas at each end. Dependent on tourists with time on their hands, it never really recovered from World War I and it closed in 1929, by which time the journey could be made much more quickly by car or bus.

After Beccles, once the meeting point for four lines, including

THE SOUTHWOLD EXPRESS — THE ENGINE JUMPS THE RAILS OWING TO EXCESSIVE SPEED, THE SKILL OF THE DRIVER ALONE SAVES ALL FROM INJURY.

▲ The erratic and decidedly slow trains on the narrow-gauge Southwold Railway inspired a series of comic cards before the line's closure in 1929. Surprisingly, at its peak in the early 1900s, the railway carried over 100,000 passengers a year as well as a fair amount of freight.

▼ In a classic 1950s scene the Yarmouth South Town to Ipswich train pulls away from Woodbridge station, with the driver keeping a good lookout. Today this journey is impossible as the line northwards from Beccles to Yarmouth is long gone.

▲ One of the main points of interest on the approach to Lowestoft is the swing bridge that connects the two sides of Oulton Broad. In 1958 a train from Ipswich with two carriages makes its way across.

◄ Nowadays Lowestoft is known for its docks and its fishing fleet, but this picture of the yacht basin is a reminder that in the early 20th century it was also a fashionable resort. Smart people, and smart yachts moored in neat rows, show us a different view of the town.

Yacht Basin, Lowestoft

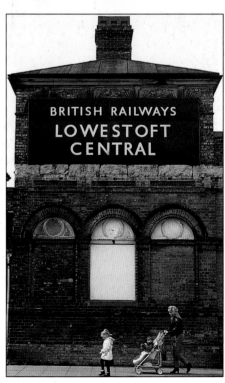

a direct route to Yarmouth, the train swings east to follow the Waveney valley through a flat landscape dominated by the presence of the sea ahead and the changing quality of light. Caravans, as ever, are the harbingers of the seaside. At one time a line went due east to Lowestoft harbour, but now the train turns north and a swing bridge takes the line across Lake Lothing, the stretch of water linking Oulton Broad to the Waveney. This is now a landscape busy with yachts and cruisers in the summer and filled with maritime life all year. Bizarrely, Oulton Broad still has two stations, North and South, a short walk apart but on different lines, and thus inaccessible from the same train. Here the train joins the Norwich line for the final approach to Lowestoft, past the docks and acres of empty sidings and dereliction. Long holiday specials and lines of fish vans were the lifeblood of the place but everything has gone now and only echoes remain of this active past. As a result Lowestoft station, much reduced, is a sad place. At least it is central, as its original name implies, and the town centre and the sea are close at hand.

▶ Lowestoft now has only one station, and that is pretty basic. In 1994, although Lowestoft North was long gone, this old British Railways enamel sign in Eastern Region colours indicated that things had once been different. At that time such survivals were not uncommon.

TO THE SEASIDE

THE VICTORIANS loved the seaside and it is to them that we owe the enduring pleasures of a day by the sea. It was the railways that made it all possible; indeed, it could be said that the railways made the British seaside. Prior to the railway age, travel to the coast was for most people tedious and expensive, and bathing was more about health than pleasure. From the 1850s it all changed, as the tentacles of the railway system reached more and more stretches of hitherto inaccessible coastline and speculative railway companies opened up lines to the sea in search of increased traffic. Some established resorts, such as Brighton, Ramsgate and Scarborough, took on a new lease of life when the trains arrived, establishing the idea of the day trip and the seaside excursion. Other places were in effect the creation of the railways, for example Cornwall and the West Country, south Wales, west Wales and north Wales, the Lancashire coast, East

▲ The faces say it all: these children interrupt their bucket and spade games to pose for the camera. It is the 1920s and, judging by the sweaters, a bit chilly. The bucket says 'A Present from the Seaside'.

Anglia and Lincolnshire, north Yorkshire and Scotland. It was the GWR that first called the south Devon resorts the English Riviera, and similar marketing ploys were dreamed up in railway offices all over the land. Competition was fierce, and promotion techniques became both intensive and sophisticated. Railways bought or built hotels in favoured resorts, and from the end of the 19th century posters, brochures, handbills and postcards were produced in huge quantities. Everyone remembers John Hassall's 'Skegness is So Bracing' poster, but that was just one of thousands of colourful images that sold to millions the idea of a seaside holiday by train.

Vol.8 No.8 August 1957

British Railways Magazine 3d

London Midland Region

travel in Rail Comfor

◄ For its August 1957 issue the staff magazine of British Railways London Midland Region featured, unusually for so conventional a publication, a pretty pin-up entitled 'The spirit of the holiday season'.

▼ It is nearly journey's end as a holiday express passes Goodrington Sands en route to Dartmouth in May 1959. The prospect of sun, sea and sand stretches ahead.

▶ This famous image was used by the Southern Railway in the 1920s.

▼ It is September 1962 and the holiday is over: a double-headed express from Bournemouth to Nottingham crosses Midford viaduct on the Somerset & Dorset line. Below it are the remains of the Camerton line, used in the filming of *The Titfield Thunderbolt*.

Driver, Where are you going, Sonny?

Little Boy, "To of course, it is such a jolly place for a holiday."

HOLIDAY CAMPS

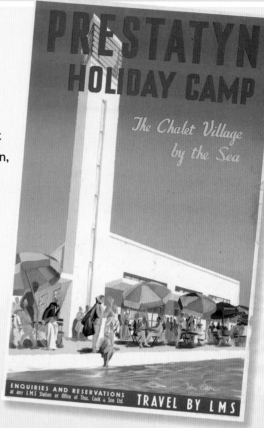

THERE IS NO DOUBT that the railways played a major part in developing the holiday trade. In many parts of Britain, resorts, some of which had been created by railway companies, relied on ever-expanding lists of excursion trains and holiday specials. Several resorts even had separate excursion stations to cater for the weight of traffic. The interwar years saw the heyday of this business, but in the 1950s competition from coaches and private cars began to undermine the railway's dominance of the holiday trade. However, one area did remain faithful to the railway, and that was the holiday camp. Butlin's started to build camps in the 1930s, and their immediate success spawned dozens more all around the coast of Britain. Sites were chosen because of their good railway access and in many places, for example Pwllheli, in Wales, and Filey, in Yorkshire, special holiday camp stations were built. By the 1970s, while holiday camps continued to flourish, they were no longer dependent upon the railway.

▼ In July 1957, hauled by a powerful old LNER K3 locomotive, a long holiday camp special sets off from Lowestoft filled with, one hopes, happy campers on their way home. Such specials were a regular feature of many summer timetables.

▲ In the 1930s, holiday camps enjoyed a smart, contemporary image and their publicity, often arranged jointly with a railway company, underlined this. Typical is this LMS poster promoting Prestatyn Holiday Camp in north Wales, which was close to the railway.

SMILING SOMERSET

BREAN SANDS HOLIDAY RESORT

▲ One of the holiday camps with its own dedicated station was Filey, on the Yorkshire coast, in this case at the end of a short branch line. Long platforms and storage sidings catered for the huge holiday specials that were still running in 1965, when this photograph was taken. It was March, so there were few passengers. Most of them seem to be looking at the old LNER locomotive.

▶ Brean Sands Holiday Resort, on the Somerset coast, was, unusually for the 1930s, not directly railway connected. However, it was easily accessed from Burnham-on-Sea or Weston-super-Mare.

BUTLIN'S SKEGNESS
Monorail

◀ During the 1960s holiday camps continued to develop, broadening their appeal and the range of their facilities. This postcard shows the monorail that Butlin's installed at their Skegness camp, as a novelty rather than as a practical means of transport. Ironically, although Skegness was railway connected, few of its clients were by this time travelling to or from the camp by the real train.

SPALDING TO YARMOUTH

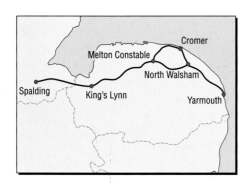

In the 1850s and 1860s East Anglia was a bit of a railway battlefield, keenly fought over by a series of ambitious companies, notably East Anglian Railways, the Eastern Counties Railway and the Eastern Union Railway. Larger companies, including the Great Northern or the Midland, were frequently lurking in the background, while in the foreground was a plethora of little local companies, often the pawns in the battle. Among these were the Lynn & Dereham, the Lynn & Fakenham, the Lynn & Sutton Bridge, the Norwich & Spalding, the Wells & Fakenham, the Yarmouth & North Norfolk and the Yarmouth & Norwich. Things became a bit clearer after 1862, with the formation of the Great Eastern Railway, which took over much of the network. Exceptions were the routes across north Norfolk, but many of these came together in 1883 as the Eastern & Midlands Railway. The geographical centre of the network was Melton Constable, a remote village where the Lynn & Fakenham company, now part of the Eastern & Midlands, had chosen to place its railway works. This remained the status quo for ten years, but the big players, the Midland and the Great Northern, were still keen to be involved, particularly if by so doing

▼ On a summer Sunday in 1958 a long holiday train en route from Spalding to Hunstanton pauses at the tiny station of Gedney, west of Sutton Bridge. Little stations such as this, serving remote communities, were a feature of the line.

▲ The spirit and atmosphere of the M&GNJR pervades this timeless scene. It is actually a modern re-creation, namely Weybourne station on the preserved North Norfolk Railway. Midway between Sheringham and Holt, Weybourne is also home to the railway's workshops and depot.

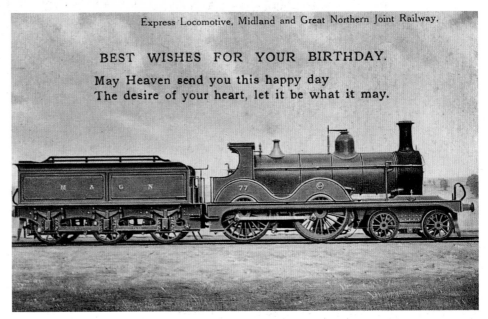

Express Locomotive, Midland and Great Northern Joint Railway.

BEST WISHES FOR YOUR BIRTHDAY.

May Heaven send you this happy day
The desire of your heart, let it be what it may.

► The M&GNJR's locomotives of the 1890s were noted for their elegance of line and attractive colour scheme, both of which are well shown on this Edwardian birthday card.

In the late 1950s a long holiday special, double-headed by two LMS freight locomotives, comes slowly into Sutton Bridge station. Much of the M&GNJR's 182-mile network was single-tracked, with passing places at the stations.

they could thwart the Great Eastern. So they formed in 1893 the Midland & Great Northern Joint Railway, to take over the interests of the Eastern & Midland and some other bits and pieces. This resulted in an independent 182-mile network, spreading from Spalding, Peterborough and King's Lynn in the west to Cromer, Yarmouth and Lowestoft in the east, with a branch to Norwich in the centre. Much of it was a classic rural railway, serving small communities and

Spl. 2,500 4/21 (564.)

Midland and Great Northern Railways Joint Committee.

FRUIT.

From LONG SUTTON.

TO

BRADFORD, G.N.R.

Via PETERBORO.'

By Passenger Train.

local needs but it was able to benefit from expanding holiday traffic to east coast resorts and useful freight connections with other networks. During its lifetime, the M&GNJR maintained a spirit of independence and its smart, light-brown coloured locomotives continued to run until 1923, when it was all absorbed into the LNER. Even then, its local character endured, and continued to do so into the era of British Railways. However, by the 1950s the death knell was tolling for this type of rural network. In many of the areas it served, road transport was cheaper and quicker. So closures began. By the end of the 1960s the M&GNJR had in effect ceased to exist, although some freight services lingered on until the 1980s. Today a short stretch from Cromer to Sheringham is the only bit to survive as part of the national network. A more significant survival, or rather revival, is the North Norfolk's preserved line from Sheringham to Holt.

▼ The M&GNJR's station for King's Lynn was South Lynn, close to the crossing of the Great Ouse on the iron girder bridge shown here. In 1958 a long train hauled, no doubt with some difficulty, by an old LMS freight locomotive waits at the distinctive M&GN somersault signals.

THE ROUTE TODAY

The flat landscape of the Wash offered few challenges to Victorian railway engineers, other than a number of crossings over various waterways. The line's original builders were generous with stations in the empty landscape east of Spalding. Often they served minute communities such as Fleet, Gedney, Walpole and Terrington, some of which lay a distance from the railway. The route from Spalding is remote, but the remains can be followed from minor roads, which regularly cross the trackbed. At Sutton Bridge, which is the first major river crossing, the M&GNJR built a large girder bridge with an opening span. This bridge was shared with a road and when the railway closed in 1959 the road took it over completely, along with a section of the trackbed to the east. The next major structure was the bridge across the Great Ouse, south of King's Lynn, but this has gone. For a while, the section east of Lynn remained in use as a freight line but this too closed years ago.

The line from Lynn to Fakenham was equally rural and remote, and maintained the pattern of serving small places a long way from the railway. Sections have

RAILWAYS AND AIRFIELDS
Ordnance Survey maps of north Norfolk and east Lincolnshire show the traces of two important features of the region's history that have now largely disappeared, railways and airfields. Both played a crucial role, yet slowly but surely are vanishing into the landscape. Both have their enthusiasts who strive to record what remains. In places along the M&GNJR routes the two come close together. There are several airfield sites in the area surrounding Fakenham: Great Massingham, West Raynham, Wood, Norton and Snoring and Sculthorpe. During World War II, when these were active units, countless airmen and women must have travelled to and from Fakenham and other nearby railway stations.

▼ In 1962 Melton Constable still had a substantial station. In many ways it was the heart of the M&GNJR network, with lines radiating in four directions. Today everything has gone, and it is hard to believe the town ever had a railway station, let alone a major railway workshop.

▲ Much of the extensive network of the M&GNJR has vanished, but in the low-lying landscape those bits that remain are easily spotted. This long embankment across the ploughed fields of early spring is near Corpusty, between Melton Constable and Aylsham.

disappeared but there is still plenty for the diligent explorer to find in the landscape. At Fakenham the M&GNJR had its own station, well to the west but called Fakenham Town regardless. The line crossed the Great Eastern's route northwards to Wells and then meandered through a more rounded and wooded landscape to Melton Constable. Of the great railway works that were constructed here, in the empty Norfolk landscape, from 1882, remarkably little remains; just a few indeterminate buildings, a massive water tower and some meaningless bits and pieces scattered around a little town whose raison d'être has vanished.

Melton was also a meeting point of four lines, west to Fakenham, east to Aylsham, south to Norwich and north to Cromer. The routes to Norwich and Aylsham are best preserved, with embankments, bridges and stations to be seen, but little remains of the route towards Cromer until just outside Holt, where it all suddenly comes back to life. A station, track and trains indicate the thriving presence of the preserved North Norfolk Railway, and in its care the memory of the M&GNJR lives on. At Sheringham the preserved railway meets the real thing which by comparison seems mean and minimal. Next comes Cromer, and more complicated history, involving three railway companies and two stations. The survivor is what was originally called Cromer Beach, an 1887 timber-framed Arts & Crafts-style building. It was this station that began the development of Cromer into a select Edwardian resort, echoes of which can be faintly detected. From Cromer there were two other routes, direct to Norwich on the Great Eastern, or a meander along the coast in the trains of the Norfolk & Suffolk Joint Railway,

which arrived in 1906. These two met at North Walsham, a busy railway junction in its heyday and still a living station on the Sheringham line.

To the west, the M&GNJR's line towards Aylsham is now defined as a footpath called the Weavers' Way. This continues to the east of North Walsham, with the footpath rejoining the railway north of Horning for a short stretch. This is a good section, with woods and waterways all around, and then it disappears into the landscape and beneath a road. From here into Yarmouth, much of the trackbed has been returned to the fields from which it came. A big bridge survives at Hemsby, now carrying a road over nothing, and a few other traces can be found. However, gone for ever are the big holiday expresses sweeping along the coast, through the suburbs and into Yarmouth Beach station, a grand terminus suitable for the resort that Yarmouth then was. Today, nothing remains of this but a few cast-iron pillars used to decorate a car park.

◀ Cromer Beach station was opened in 1887 and brought the resort to life. The M&GNJR made the most of this smart station, which at the time of this photograph was the eastern terminus of their network. Today the buildings survive, in other uses, and trains still come to Cromer station.

▲ Iron pillars decorated with the initials of the companies that built Yarmouth Beach station now stand in a car park as a kind of memorial to a station of which there is today no other trace. This one commemorates the Midland & Great Northern.

▲ A surprising survivor is this bridge plate, set into the stonework of a busy road bridge near Hemsby. The trackbed that ran beneath it and across the surrounding fields having been obliterated, the bridge now carries the traffic over nothing.

◀ This Edwardian view of Sheringham's High Street has plenty of period detail, conveying the style and atmosphere of this smart little seaside resort largely created by the M&GNJR. Sheringham's elegant station is still in use, by the preserved North Norfolk Railway, and the town is connected to the national network via a branch from Norwich.

▲ In the 1950s much of the network was still intact and busy with both expresses and local services. This is the stopping train from Yarmouth Beach to North Walsham, seen here departing from Caister-on-Sea, a station virtually on the beach and famous for its holiday camps.

▶ This card of Yarmouth's Britannia Pier was posted in 1906, at the peak of the development of this Norfolk coast resort. The railways played a crucial role in that process, and celebrated that by producing promotional postcards. Yarmouth Beach station was the starting point for many a holiday visit.

THE BRITANNIA PIER, Gt. YARMOUTH.

ROYAL TRAINS

QUEEN VICTORIA first travelled by train on 13 June 1842, and she enjoyed the experience. She used royal trains extensively throughout her reign, particularly on journeys to Osborne, on the Isle of Wight, and Balmoral, in Scotland. Carriages were lavish and comfortable, specially built by various railway companies. From the late 1840s they were fitted with a lavatory. The organization of royal train journeys was complex, involving different companies and compounded by security concerns and the Queen's insistence on a 40mph maximum speed. Subsequent monarchs continued to use royal trains regularly, making the most of new vehicles as they were introduced and travelling at normal speeds. The royal family always paid to use the trains, and invoices indicate that even the dogs were charged for.

Today the royal train, completely refurbished in 1985, is used from time to time, though regularly threatened with the axe. It survives simply because it still offers a high degree of comfort, security and privacy.

▼ A lucky enthusiast is on the spot to film the royal train passing Wormald Green, near Harrogate, in May 1967. The carriages and the Jubilee class locomotive 'Alberta' suggest an earlier period.

▲ The LNWR built a new royal train for Edward VII and Queen Alexandra, with a notably contemporary look to its interior decoration and fittings, and every modern convenience. Justifiably proud, the company displayed it in a series of official postcards.

▲ On a summer's day in 1986 the recently refurbished royal train passed through Llandrindod Wells on the Central Wales line, hauled by an immaculate class 47 diesel.

▼ This card from the LNWR official series shows the light, spacious and informal style of Queen Alexandra's sleeping compartment on her new royal train.

▼ This timetable, issued to passengers on a royal train in May 1955, shows the meticulous planning involved in a royal journey, including the overnight stop.

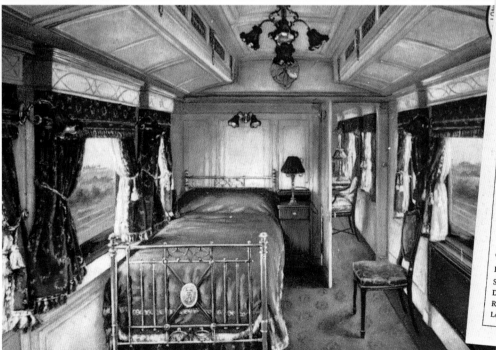

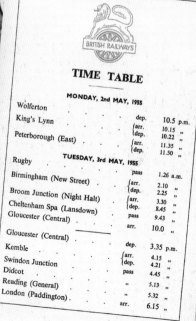

BRITISH RAILWAYS

TIME TABLE

MONDAY, 2nd MAY, 1955

Wolferton	dep.	10.5 p.m.
King's Lynn	{ arr.	10.15 "
	{ dep.	10.22 "
Peterborough (East)	{ arr.	11.35 "
	{ dep.	11.50 "

TUESDAY, 3rd MAY, 1955

Rugby	pass	1.26 a.m.
Birmingham (New Street)	{ arr.	2.10 "
	{ dep.	2.25 "
Broom Junction (Night Halt)	{ arr.	3.30 "
	{ dep.	8.45 "
Cheltenham Spa (Lansdown)	pass	9.43 "
Gloucester (Central)	arr.	10.0 "
Gloucester (Central)	dep.	3.35 p.m.
Kemble	pass	4.15 "
Swindon Junction	{ arr.	4.15 "
	{ dep.	4.21 "
Didcot	pass	4.45 "
Reading (General)	"	5.13 "
London (Paddington)	"	5.32 "
	arr.	6.15 "

Central England

BUXTON TO ASHBOURNE AND HIGH PEAK JUNCTION

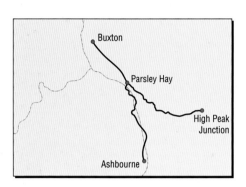

Two rival railways arrived in Buxton in 1863, the LNWR and the Midland. At the insistence of the Duke of Devonshire, who owned much of the town and wanted to ensure that modern developments were in keeping with Buxton's architectural traditions, two matching stations were built side by side, handsome stone-built train sheds with large semi-circular windows in the gable ends. This striking and, in railway terms, unique pair of buildings was destroyed, except for one gable end left standing in a pointless way, when it all closed in 1967.

Mineral lines and later additions complicated the railway map around Buxton, notably a route southwards to Ashbourne, opened by the LNWR in 1892. This met the existing branch to Ashbourne, built by the North Staffordshire Railway from Stoke and Uttoxeter in 1852, and enabled trains to run from Buxton through to Burton and beyond. The upper section of this LNWR route, from Hindlow, south

▼ A famous spa resort at least since the 18th century, Buxton enjoyed enormous popularity during the Victorian and Edwardian periods, thanks in part to the railway. Theatres and the Pavilion were added to the town's existing attractions and, at the time of this card, it was a very smart place indeed.

▲ An ancient tradition of many villages of the Derbyshire Peak district is the dressing of local wells with images and patterns made from flowers. Several of these villages are close to this line, for example Tissington.

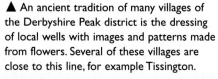

THE PAVILION. BUXTON.

▶ The Derbyshire scenery was perennially popular, and the railways that crossed it did all they could to encourage tourist traffic. This official LNWR card, issued before 1914, shows Raven's Tor in Bradford Dale, a spot accessible from Parsley Hay station, on the Buxton to Ashbourne route.

RAVEN'S TOR, BRADFORD DALE.
PARSLEY HAY STN. L. & N.W. RAILWAY.

▼ Stone traffic was the justification for a number of lines built through the demanding Derbyshire landscape, and the importance of this continues today. In this 1961 photograph, a limestone train heads northwards towards Buxton, hauled by an elderly LMS goods locomotive.

The Lion Rock, Dovedale

▲ The Tissington Trail is one of the most popular of the cycleways created along former railway lines, as this photograph indicates. The 14-mile route is an exciting mixture of glorious scenery and railway history.

◄ The LNWR issued a great number of postcards before 1914 to promote tourist traffic on its Derbyshire routes, and many famous places were featured, whether they were on a railway or not. The Lion Rock, Dovedale, is to the west of Ashbourne.

of Buxton, to Parsley Hay, used the track of one of Britain's most remarkable railways, the Cromford & High Peak. Conceived originally as a canal to link the Cromford Canal to the Peak Forest Canal at Whaley Bridge, this was built as a railway from 1830, but canal engineering determined its nature. Over its 33 miles, it climbed 976 feet from Cromford and descended 745 feet to Whaley Bridge. The route was winding, following contour lines, there were three tunnels, long lengths of stone-faced embankments and, where there would have been flights of locks, there were nine inclined planes, up which wagons were dragged on chains or ropes powered by stationary steam engines. Wagons were initially pulled by horses on the level sections, but steam locomotives were introduced from 1833. Primary traffic was limestone but there were limited passenger facilities until 1876. From the 1860s, when the LNWR took over, the route was straightened and simplified, and the number of inclines reduced to seven. However, the process of travel remained slow and complex along a railway that was essentially a pre-Victorian concept. What is even more remarkable is that a large part of the route remained in use until the mid-1960s, when this veritable antique was finally abandoned, with the lines to Ashbourne. Buxton still has a station, but the connecting line south

▼ Parts of the Cromford & High Peak line, by then an extraordinary anachronism, were still in use in 1966. Here, an Austerity tank rounds Gotham Curve. The stone-faced embankment is typical of the line.

to Matlock and Cromford went at the same time. Peak Rail plan to re-open it as a preserved line. South of Buxton, small parts of the network survive, serving the local quarries.

THE ROUTE TODAY

Today the major parts of the route, from High Peak Junction near Cromford north to Downlow (the High Peak Trail) and from Parsley Hay south to Ashbourne (the Tissington Trail), form a long-distance cycle track, one of the best in Britain. In total it offers over 30 miles of cycling through glorious Derbyshire scenery, along well-surfaced tracks, and with countless opportunities to admire the extraordinary achievements of the early 19th-century railway builders, to whom every obstacle was merely a challenge to be overcome. Inclines, tunnels, bridges and embankments survive, along with an engine house, goods sheds, warehouses and other relics. For those not excited by railway trails, there are classic Derbyshire villages, Hartington and Tissington, and the eternal pleasures of the landscape.

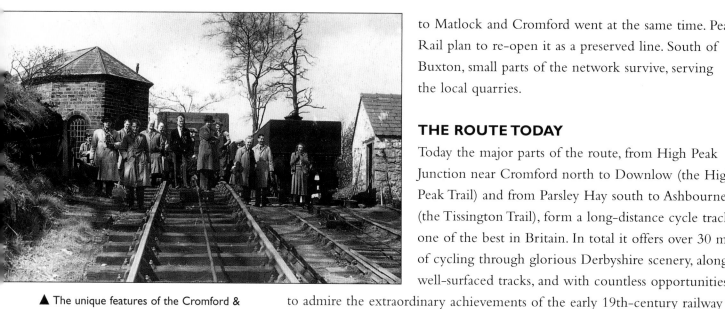

▲ The unique features of the Cromford & High Peak Railway drew many visitors while it was still in operation. Here, a group from a visiting rail tour pose at the top of Sheep Pasture Incline in September 1953.

▼ In its last years the Cromford & High Peak was much visited by photographers keen to capture its unique qualities. This was taken in 1966 by Ivo Peters, a well-known railway photographer. The locomotive's crew look as if they have already posed a number of times.

THE MARKET PLACE, ASHBOURNE

◀ Ashbourne received its first railway in 1854, and the line from Buxton arrived 40 years later. From that point onwards, this traditional Derbyshire market town became a popular resort and a useful base for visits to the Peak District. This card shows the market place in about 1910.

◀ The High Peak Trail, a cycleway along 17 miles of the former Cromford & High Peak Railway, is an easy way to enjoy the landscape of the Peak District while exploring the visible legacy of the engineering of the Industrial Revolution.

ENGINE SHEDS

WHEN BRITISH RAILWAYS was formed in 1947, it inherited a fleet of over 20,000 steam locomotives, scattered all over the network. The daily maintenance of these took place in an equally diverse collection of depots and yards with engine or running sheds, where locomotives could be stored, serviced, coaled, watered, emptied of ash and turned. At this point they were taken on shed, ready for work. Mainline sheds could handle large numbers of locomotives, and were equipped with turntables, ash and maintenance pits, watering and coaling facilities, the latter often mechanized, as well as workshops and offices. At the other end of the spectrum, a branch-line terminus might have a little shed for one small locomotive, a water tower and a pile of coal to be loaded by hand. There were two standard forms of sheds: the long one with parallel tracks, glazed roof with smoke vents, and sometimes access from both ends; and the roundhouse type, with tracks radiating from a central turntable. The first of these, built at Derby in 1840, held 30 locomotives. This type became popular even though the layout restricted locomotive movement. Initially built of stone and brick with cast-iron roof supports, sheds were later made of concrete and steel. Few survive today and rarely in an original form.

▼ Locomotives on shed at Tebay await banking duties on the West Coast main line in the 1960s. This was a classic example of the linear type of shed, with water tower.

▶ One of the most famous roundhouse sheds was at Swindon. In this atmospheric 1920s shot, taken from the central turntable, Castles and a King await the call to duty.

▲ Even miniature railways need sheds. This is on the Ravenglass & Eskdale Railway in Cumbria, with locomotives on shed in 1969.

◄ At Inverness the Highland Railway had a grand horseshoe-shaped roundhouse with 34 radiating tracks. The magnificent triumphal arch over the entrance track is actually the water tower. Seen here still in use in 1957, it was all demolished in 1962.

RAILWAY WORKS

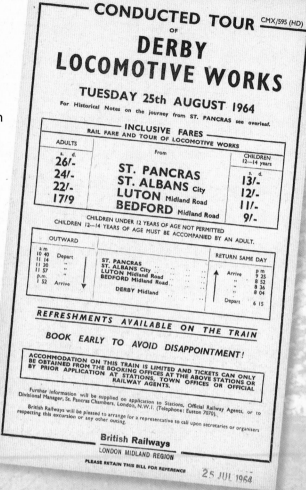

THE FIRST FACTORY set up to manufacture railway locomotives was opened by Robert Stephenson in 1823. Many others quickly followed. Famous names among the independent operators soon in the business included Vulcan Foundry, Sharp Stewart, Avonside, Hunslet, Beyer Peacock, and Andrew Barclay. The railway companies, too, built factories at their construction and maintenance works: during the Victorian period locomotives were being made in at least 25 works, the best known being Darlington, Doncaster, Derby, Crewe, Swindon and Ashford. In 1900 British manufacturers were producing some 2,000 locomotives a year, selling them all over the world. Other companies specialized in rolling stock. Following the 1923 grouping, some rationalization took place, a pattern followed after the setting up of British Railways. By now the emphasis was on diesel and electric traction, and the last mainline steam locomotive, 'Evening Star', left the Swindon works in 1960. Today few railway vehicles are built in Britain, but the independent operators have opened new maintenance facilities.

◀ Many railway works focused on maintenance rather than building new vehicles. During its lifetime, apart from regular maintenance, a locomotive may have several refurbishments. This photograph shows class 31 and class 50 diesel locomotives, some dating to the 1960s, being totally rebuilt at the Doncaster works in 1984.

▶ During World War II many women replaced men in the workshops: in 1942 this machinist was photographed working for the Southern Railway.

▲ Major railway works were massive operations, employing thousands of people, and able to undertake every aspect of the building and maintenance of trains. One of the best known was Swindon, built by the GWR. Here, 'King Edward VI' undergoes an overhaul in 1956.

▶ In 1937 one hundred new steam locomotives were built at the Darlington works for the LNER, part of a major modernization programme. Here, some of the wheel-sets for these locomotives are assembled and inspected.

SHREWSBURY TO NEWPORT

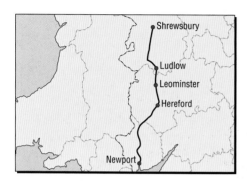

The journey from Shrewsbury to Newport is a voyage through history, an exploration of the Marches, the borderlands that mark the boundary between England and Wales, disputed since the days of the Romans. It is, as a result, a route marked by great castles, or the remains of them, most notably at Shrewsbury, Ludlow and Newport. By the time the railways came, boundary disputes on a national scale were a thing of the past. Instead, there were many border towns, still slumbering in a pre-industrial age, that wanted to share in the prosperity of the early 19th century. Early railway schemes, therefore, had plenty of supporters and some industrial lines and tramways were being built in the 1820s. Plans for local lines followed, but the need for a major north–south route soon became apparent. In 1846 a 51-mile line from Shrewsbury to Hereford was authorized but work did not start until 1850. The first passengers were carried three years later, by which time the southern part of the route was also nearing completion. The builder of this was the Newport, Abergavenny & Hereford Railway, initially part of a much more ambitious scheme called the Welsh Midland Railway, which was never to be completed. By 1854 the whole route was open and it soon became the backbone of a network of lesser lines that connected with it or crossed it. At each end were major rail centres, Shrewsbury and

▼ Shrewsbury's great neo-Tudor station looks much the same today as it does in this early 20th-century view. Its style was determined by nearby medieval and 17th-century buildings, notably the castle and the old school. Completed in 1849, it was enlarged in 1855 by the same architect, T M Penson, and then again in 1903, without destroying its integrity. It stands in a loop of the Severn, at the centre of the town.

Shrewsbury Station

▶ Many of the stations on the route were minor halts serving tiny communities. All of these were closed from the 1960s. Typical was All Stretton Halt, just north of Church Stretton, seen here in 1957 with a stopping train from Shrewsbury to Hereford – a large GWR Hall class locomotive, three carriages and probably not many passengers.

▼ In the summer of 1988 a typical modern Marches line train on its way to Shrewsbury follows the winding route of the railway through a glorious Shropshire landscape. This is seen near Marshwood, to the north of Craven Arms and close to the former junction with a long-closed line to Wellington and the Severn valley.

THE CASTLE & DINHAM BRIDGE
LUDLOW

▲ A classic small town, and perennially popular with visitors since the arrival of the railway, Ludlow has featured on thousands of postcards over the last century. This is a typical Edwardian view, showing Dinham Bridge and the castle ruins.

▼ On a June Sunday in 1961, Hereford station is busy and steam is still king. A smart Castle class locomotive departs with its train, the lunchtime Shrewsbury to Cardiff service, while another, perhaps London-bound, awaits its turn. Hereford station is another decorative, 1850s Tudor-style building.

Newport, and in between there were important junctions at Craven Arms, Leominster, Hereford, Abergavenny and Pontypool. It therefore became an important through route for both freight and passengers and a busy connecting line between south Wales and the Midlands. As such, much of it was used jointly by the GWR and the LNWR, although it was mostly in GWR territory. The pattern was maintained by the GWR and LMS after 1923. In the British Railways era, traffic steadily declined, and in the 1960s most branches and connecting lines went. Today, though still important as a direct link between south and north Wales and the Midlands, it is in effect a country railway with passenger services in the hands of diesel railcars. The only connections are at Craven Arms, the start of the Heart of Wales route, and Hereford, terminus for the line from London via Oxford and Worcester.

THE JOURNEY

The starting point is Shrewsbury's magnificent Tudor-style station, designed by T M Penson and completed in 1849 as a joint terminus for the Shrewsbury & Birmingham and Shrewsbury & Chester companies. Its decorative richness sets the tone for a journey notable for its architecture as well as its landscape.

Highlights include Shrewsbury itself, whose castle is visible from the train as it crosses the river Severn; the gaunt summit of Caer Caradoc and its Roman fort nearby; the distant view of the Long Mynd; the wooded Onny valley; and, near Craven Arms, 13th-century Stokesay Castle, the classic medieval blend of domestic and military architecture. Another castle awaits the train at Ludlow, one of England's best small towns, set beside the Teme. Next is Leominster, a wool town with plenty of 18th-century buildings, and then the landscape becomes more open, scattered with the spires and towers of village churches. Hereford's cathedral can be seen, but not much else in that city as the station is well away from the centre. The line now enters Wales, with distant Black Mountain views to Abergavenny, a pleasant market town a long way from its station. From here, the railway follows the Usk valley south to Pontypool and the start of more industrial surroundings that stretch to Cwmbran. The rural landscape returns as the line curves past Roman Caerleon, and then it joins the main line from London and Bristol for the final entry into Newport. A handsome iron bridge carries the railway over the Usk right by the ruins of the medieval castle, an architectural conjunction that epitomizes the line.

▲ By 1965 services were already much reduced and diesel railcars were taking over, setting the pattern for the future. This is Llanfihangel, to the north of Abergavenny.

▼ In the late 1980s a class 50 diesel in Network SouthEast livery hauls its train across the Usk bridge prior to entering Newport station. To the left are the remains of the medieval castle.

GOODS

For a century from the 1860s, freight revenues on Britain's railways were at least 30 per cent higher than passenger income. Indeed, many companies depended upon the carriage of freight for their survival. Goods trains were the backbone of the national network. Railways were vital for the transport of bulk commodities, notably coal, stone, clay, cement, bricks, oil, petrol and chemicals, and a whole range of materials relating to agriculture and food, including fruit and vegetables, milk, fish, livestock, grain and fertilizers, all usually transported in dedicated wagons. Equally important was the carriage and distribution of a huge range of domestic, commercial and industrial products, which included a national parcels service. For a century from the 1850s everybody relied on the railways to transport and deliver everything. Most stations had goods sidings and the visit of the local pick-up goods train was a regular event. All this was made possible by detailed record keeping and by a nationwide network of freight yards and marshalling centres. Today, after years of decline, only bulk cargoes and container traffic survive.

GREAT WESTERN RAILWAY. (999-1)

From _Gweshy_

TO _Weston Wharf._

_G. W_

ROUTE VIA _____ RAILWAY

Date _14/5_ 1924. Train ____

Wagon No. _944016_

Total No. Sheets

Total No. Ropes

Consignee _R. E. Kirkpatrick Esq_

Contents _Firewood Sleepers_

500,000 W 34 Spl. 5/23 B.

▲ The smooth running of the freight business required accurate labelling of every wagon to identify the destination, contents and client. In the pre-computer era these were prepared, recorded and attached to the wagon by hand. Every journey required a label, to ensure the wagon reached the correct destination.

◄ At various points in the network, huge marshalling yards organized the movement of wagons and their assembly into the right position, in the right train. This is Toton, near Nottingham, in 1947.

BRITISH RAILWAYS
.... REGION

B.R. 11223

FOR REPAIRS

From ....

To .... Yard

.... Yard

AT .... WORKSOP

.... Station

Date ....

.... Examiner

Any unauthorised person obscuring or removing this Card will render himself liable to Criminal Prosecution

▲ Until the 1960s the local pick-up goods train was a familiar sight and the constant movement of assorted railway wagons was the heart of the system. Typical is this mixed goods train photographed in 1950 on the Somerset & Dorset line near Cole, with milk tankers and parcel wagons under the control of an elderly 0-6-0 goods locomotive.

▲ The maintenance of hundreds of thousands of goods wagons was a mammoth task, requiring most detailed record keeping. The system, established in the 19th century and still current in the British Railways era, relied on the accurate use of wagon labels.

► The railways were early users of containers for simplifying the trans-shipment and delivery of a wide range of goods. In the 1950s there were thousands in use, and many of them could be interchanged between road and rail. Here a consignment of bicycles is being delivered from a specialized rail/road container.

RAIL CENTRE: STOKE-ON-TRENT

A GLANCE AT ANY EARLY 20th-century railway map reveals Stoke-on-Trent as the hub of a small but unusually complex network, much of which was built by the North Staffordshire Railway. This intensely independent and highly localized company, often known as 'a small octopus', was established in 1846 and by the early 1850s much of its network was complete, including lines to Crewe, Uttoxeter, Macclesfield, Stafford, Burton-on-Trent and Ashbourne. These offered connections with other railways, making journeys possible to Manchester, Derby, London and elsewhere.

OLD MORETON HALL, CHESHIRE

The black and white splendour of Old Moreton Hall was greatly appreciated in the late Victorian period, thanks to a new interest in historic country houses. Although not served directly by NSR trains, it was easily accessible from a number of local stations, including Congleton, Lawton and Mow Cop. The NSR did much to encourage enthusiasm for such local landmarks. The Hall is now owned by the National Trust.

ECCLESTON FERRY, CHESTER

The NSR's line to Crewe opened up a connection to Chester, a walled city popular with visitors since the Middle Ages. A well-known local beauty spot was Eccleston Ferry, where boating on the river Dee was on offer. This card, written in 1909, indicates in its message the contemporary confidence in the post office: 'Tell your brothers I will call this evening.'

Later additions included a line to Market Drayton and the famous Potteries loop line, a precursor of the modern metro network opened in 1875. There was also a wealth of colliery and freight lines, reflecting the extensive local coalfields and the clay and iron and steel industries. The North Staffordshire Railway, and its dark red locomotives, continued to operate until July 1923, when it was absorbed into the LMS. Since the 1960s much of the old NSR network has vanished, leaving only the main lines to London, Manchester, Crewe and Derby.

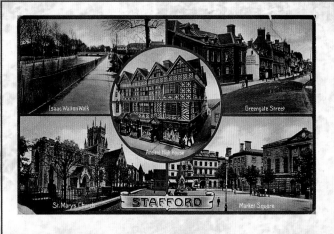

STAFFORD

This 1913 postcard shows that Stafford, not a notably attractive town even in the Edwardian era, was doing its best to draw its share of visitors. Izaac Walton was born here in 1593 and was baptised in the church shown on the card. Situated on the main line northwards to Crewe, Stafford was by the 1840s accessible from Stoke via Stone, a remarkable Jacobean-style station designed by the NSR's charismatic architect, H A Hunt.

MACCLESFIELD

Long famous as a centre of the silk trade, Macclesfield was by the late Victorian period an intriguing mixture of medieval streets, 18th-century elegance and huge textile mills. This old card shows mills and terrace houses against the backdrop of the hills that frame the Bolin valley in which the town sits. The elevated route of the railway is in the centre. There were two ways to Macclesfield from Stoke, one up the main line to Manchester via Congleton, and the other a more roundabout and scenic journey via Leek and Bosley, on the northern part of the Churnet Valley line. There was also an indirect route, via the Potteries loop line, Biddulph and Congleton Junction. Today, only the Manchester main line survives, but the view of Macclesfield from the train is still exciting.

Stoke in 1911, the hub of the NSR

STOKE-ON-TRENT

LEEK

Rudyard Lake, a well-known beauty spot near Leek, was served directly by trains from Stoke. It was much promoted by the NSR as a destination for day and weekend trips. This card, posted in 1913 by Florrie from Newcastle-under-Lyme, who had been staying in a cottage in Rudyard for a few days, underlines the essentially local appeal of the lake, its setting and its boating facilities.

BURTON-ON-TRENT

A town devoted to brewing since the Middle Ages, Burton became an important centre of industry in the 19th century thanks to the Midland Railway, whose ambitions provided its many railway connections. At the same time, as this card suggests, Burton was keen to present itself as a modern town with plenty to attract visitors, notably the banks of the Trent. The Town Hall, shown here, was given to Burton by the brewer Michael Bass, later Lord Burton. The writer, staying nearby in 1919, says, inevitably: 'what lovely weather, we are having a nice time.' The railway line from Stoke was via Uttoxeter and Tutbury. This closed in the 1960s, so a direct journey is impossible today.

FUNERAL TRAINS

THE FUNERAL TRAIN, marking the final journey of notable figures, and in particular members of the royal family, is one of many special services developed during the 19th century. After Queen Victoria's death at Osborne House, on the Isle of Wight, in January 1901, her body was transported to the mainland on the royal yacht. From the private station at Gosport, she then travelled to London for the lying-in-state and funeral.

Another rail journey followed, for the burial at Windsor. In less exalted circumstances, coffins were frequently transported by train, on regular services, usually in the guard's van. In 1854 a large cemetery was set up at Brookwood, near Woking, in Surrey, by the London Necropolis Company. A funeral train ran there daily from the grand Waterloo Necropolis station, where mourners could gather before boarding the train. This soon proved popular, and services were maintained until World War II.

S 2409   THE STATION, BROOKWOOD CEMETERY.

▲ The railway funeral is staging a comeback, with a few preserved lines now offering special trains and services. The Midland Railway Centre in Debyshire, in conjunction with Peace Burials of Ormskirk, offers a package that includes a wicker coffin, a steam-hauled final journey and a burial spot within sight of the railway. Many enthusiasts have their ashes scattered by the line or put into the engine's firebox.

◄ In the early 1920s a funeral train from Waterloo steams slowly into one of the two special stations at Brookwood – an unexpected scene to find on a postcard. The Necropolis Company supplied the hearse vans but services were operated initially by the LSWR and later by the Southern Railway.

Battle of Britain' Class Locomotive, "Winston Churchill" BY PERMISSION OF BRITISH RAILWAYS.
3365

▲ ◄ ▲ Sir Winston Churchill, who died in January 1965, was probably the last Briton to have a great railway funeral. After its journey up the Thames, his coffin was loaded on to the train at Waterloo station, watched by members of his family. The Pullman train, headed by the Battle of Britain class locomotive that carried his name, then headed westwards, through the rain, towards Oxfordshire. No. 34051 'Winston Churchill' was subsequently preserved and now forms part of the National Railway Museum collection at York.

► Other monarchs followed the precedent set by Queen Victoria and were carried to their burial places in royal funeral trains, though generally with less complex journeys than hers. King Edward VII, Queen Victoria's son, died only nine years after her, in 1910. Here, on 20 May, crowds line the track as his royal funeral train passes through Ealing, in west London, on its journey to Windsor.

The Royal Funeral Train passing through Ealing.

Photo Wakefields Ealing. Copyright.

Wales

SHREWSBURY TO SWANSEA

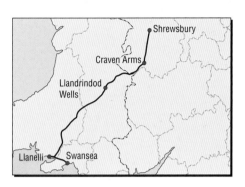

The route from Shrewsbury to Swansea, one of Britain's premier rail journeys, is in reality a glorious anachronism whose continued survival is little short of miraculous. Today the single carriage takes four hours to cover 121 miles and serves 27 stations, many remote beyond belief. There is very little traffic but the landscape is an unrolling panorama of delight. Anyone enjoying this unusual experience must wonder how the line came to be built. It is a complex story.

By the 1830s there was a network of horse-drawn railways in south Wales linking the pits to the coal ports, one of the most important of which was Llanelli. From here the Llanelly Railway & Dock Company built a line northwards in stages, reaching Pontardulais in 1839, Llandeilo in 1857 and ultimately Llandovery. At this point, passenger services were started on the line, supported by the GWR. In the meantime, things were stirring at the other end, with the opening in 1861 of the Knighton Railway's line from Craven Arms. This was supported by the GWR's

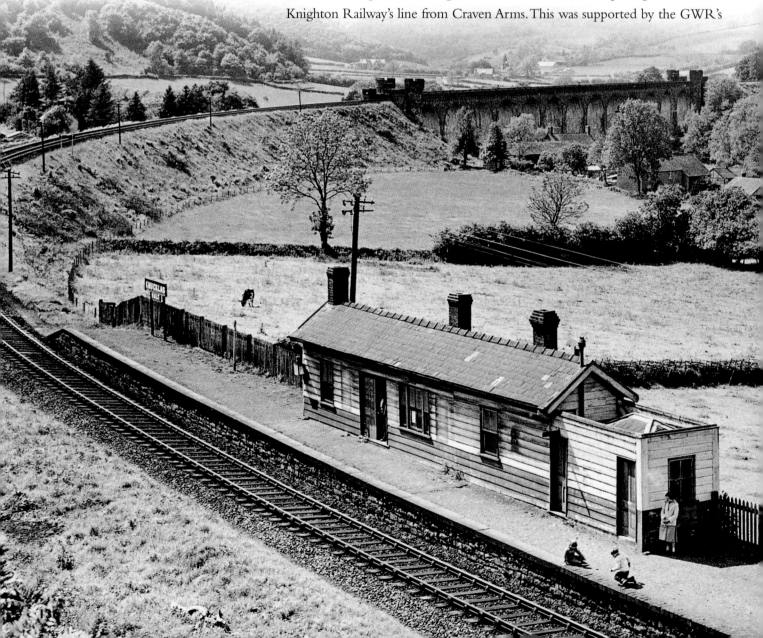

▶ With its battlements, arrow slits and 13 arches of rough-hewn stone, Knucklas is one of the best viaducts in Britain. Apparently inspired by local medieval castles and completed in 1864, it crosses a little tributary of the Teme, ringed by glorious hills. This extravagant folly was built to satisfy the tastes of a local landowner.

▶ By 1960, when this pamphlet was issued, the line was declining and efforts were being made to encourage traffic. Cheap day tickets were offered (Knucklas to Knighton, 1s 0d return), along with circular tours and party outings, including juveniles aged under 16 in groups of eight or more – inconceivable today!

PLEASE RETAIN THIS PAMPHLET FOR REFERENCE

WESTERN REGION

CHEAP DAY TICKETS

EACH DAY
(including SUNDAYS WHERE TRAIN SERVICE IS IN OPERATION)
Commencing 1st JANUARY, 1960
AND UNTIL FURTHER NOTICE

FROM
OSWESTRY

Welshpool	Newtown	Aberystwyth
Moat Lane	Llanidloes	Builth Wells
Aberdovey	Barmouth	Pwllheli
Knighton		Llandrindod Wells

Llanwrtyd Wells
AND INTERMEDIATE STATIONS

THIS PUBLICATION CANCELS ALL PREVIOUS ANNOUNCEMENTS
Paddington Station, W.2.   J. R. HAMMOND,
January, 1960.   General Manager.

◀ It is a summer's day at Knucklas Halt, and not much is happening. Two boys play on the platform, watched by their mother. Their cycles are ready to be loaded onto the train when it arrives. Another lady peeps out of the waiting room. The station has seen better days but its setting is magnificent, with a fine view of the viaduct nestled in the hills.

This line's success in Victorian Britain has much to do with the number of spa towns along the route. Mineral water springs at Llandrindod Wells were known to the Romans but it was in the 19th century that this remote spa town became fashionable. After the arrival of the railway the town could attract some 100,000 visitors a year, hotels flourished and the town's population rose from 250 to 2,000. There were through trains from London and other parts of Britain. Other spas offered different waters and treatments: chalybeate, saline and sulphur springs at Builth Wells, sulphur springs at Llanwrtyd Wells, barium chloride springs at Llangammarch Wells. Now the fashion has passed and these remote little towns can look back with wonder at their popularity in the great age of the train.

▶ Llandindrod Wells on a sunny day can still be a cheerful and busy station, as this 1994 photograph indicates. The rather unusual glazed canopy was added during restoration

▼ It is June 1964 and the Shrewsbury train pulls in to Llandrindod Wells. A few passengers are waiting, some with their bicycles. At this time the other side of the station, where a member of staff has left his motorbike, was closed and overgrown. Today the station has undergone some restoration and both sides are in use.

great rival, the LNWR, which was keen to open a route to the lucrative south Wales coal mines. Another company, the Central Wales, extended this to Llandrindod Wells in 1865, and yet another, the Central Wales Extension Railway, finally filled the gap to Llandovery three years later. All, of course, were backed by the LNWR. There was a brief war between the two rivals, but agreement was reached and from the 1870s the GWR and LNWR in effect shared the line, which became a primary freight route. This pattern of traffic survived until the 1950s. Since then the decline has been steady, with only a few, little-used passenger services keeping the route open. The Swansea–York mail, the last 'freight' of any kind ended in 1964. First threatened with closure in 1962, the passenger-only line somehow survives.

THE JOURNEY

It is a glorious, leisurely journey, with a diversity of landscape and wildlife; the train is a good platform for spotting buzzards and even the red kite. Despite its Heart of Wales marketing tag, part of the route, as far as Knighton and the river Teme, is in England. Bilingual signs make clear the train's arrival in Wales and, in any case,

passengers and crew are often
Welsh-speakers. Some stations, with
names difficult to pronounce and
hard to find on a map, are request
stops. Passengers, and stops, are
often few and far between. There
are many farm crossings, through
which the train crawls, and plenty of
features that hint at the line's former
grandeur and the ambitions behind
its building. Richly detailed stations
quietly decay, once-flourishing
goods and livestock yards lie derelict.

From Craven Arms, Shropshire's
gently undulating green fields and
timber-framed farms give way to a
more dramatic landscape of winding river valleys and distant views of hills. It is a
remote and empty landscape punctuated by little old-fashioned towns and villages,
many of which have seen better days. A number were spa towns, making the line
very popular with the Victorians, who travelled here in great numbers to take the
waters. There are two great viaducts, picturesque Knucklas, with castellations and
arrow slits, and the curving Cynghordy, as well as the long tunnel beneath the Sugar
Loaf, which emphasizes the rugged nature of the terrain. After the tunnel the train
starts its long descent into a wide panorama that spans the Black Mountains and the
Brecon Beacons, and thence into softer, wooded valleys. Until the 1960s there were
junctions with other routes, at Builth and Llandeilo, but these have vanished, along

LAWN OF PUMP HOUSE
LLANGAMMARCH WELLS.

▲ The LNWR promoted this line to increase
leisure use, the emphasis being on the spa
towns. This official card, showing croquet on
the lawns of the Pump Room, Llangammarch
Wells, has a delightful period charm.

▼ At Builth Road the line crossed the old
Cambrian Railways route through central
Wales via Caersws, Llanidloes, Rhayader and
Brecon. Builth itself was on this line, well to
south of the crossing, but there was a halt
here, with a hydraulic lift to the station above.
Builth Road station closed in 1962 and this
1964 picture shows demolition under way.

▲ Sand from the beach, just to the right, has spread across the track at Swansea Bay station. In May 1964 trainspotters on the bridge note the former GWR tank 3671 as it pulls away the stopping train from Swansea Victoria to Pontardulais.

▼ In the 1950s there was still plenty of freight traffic. Working hard, a mixed goods nears the end of the long climb to Sugar Loaf tunnel. Included in the train are some of the small containers designed for easy transfer between road and rail.

with the direct line to Swansea's Victoria station, the line's original terminus. The train now goes to Llanelli, through the industrial Lougher valley, and then across a marshy landscape towards the sea. At Llanelli, it reverses along the main line into Swansea. For this short stretch, the train is often full.

The continued, if uncertain existence of the Heart of Wales line gives a real sense of 1950s train travel. Line support groups, regional tourism, marketing campaigns, pretty flowery stations, walkers and, so the rumour goes, marginal parliamentary seats on the route help to keep it open. This is about the true experience of railway travel. There is a much quicker route from Shrewsbury to Swansea, via Newport.

▼ In the summer of 1960 the 10.25 to Shrewsbury is ready to leave Swansea Victoria. By then this two-platform terminus was rather basic, but still boasted its delicate iron train shed.

F.A. CUP 3rd ROUND

HUDDERSFIEL
TOWN
v
WEST HA

BUFFET CA

SPORTS SPECIALS

MOST MASS SPECTATOR sports were developed by the Victorians, with the railways playing a major role. The popularity of football soared after the establishment of the League and the Championship, both of which encouraged the large-scale movement of spectators by train – the famous Cup Final of 1923 at Wembley Stadium attracted over 200,000 fans, most of whom travelled by train. Football grounds, which were often in city centres, were usually located near railways; some had their own station, for example West Bromwich Albion's Hawthorn Halt. Football specials, started by railway companies in the 1880s, were immensely successful until the 1990s, when escalating vandalism and drunkenness brought them to an end.

Horse racing is a much older sport than football but it was to the railways that it owed its rapid expansion in the 19th century. Racecourses near railways flourished, and some, including Newbury, Cheltenham and Newmarket, had dedicated stations. Horses were transported by rail in horseboxes until the 1970s. Race day excursions were a significant source of income, and even today Waterloo is awash with smart hats in Ascot week and on Derby Day.

LMS C 71/R

ASSOCIATION FOOTBALL
First Division
BLACKPOOL v **CHARLTON ATHLETIC**
Good Friday, April 15th
At BLOOMFIELD ROAD, BLACKPOOL.
Kick-off 3 p.m.

THURSDAY NIGHT, APRIL 14
DAY EXCURSION
TO
BLACKPOOL
(NORTH)

FROM	TIME OF DEPARTURE	RETURN FARE (Third Class)	
		s.	d.
LONDON (EUSTON)	Night 1.30		
BLACKPOOL (NORTH) arr.	a.m. 6.10	**15**	**9**

BOOKINGS ALSO FROM SUBURBAN STATIONS AS SHOWN OVERLEAF.

RETURN ARRANGEMENTS.

Passengers holding One-day Tickets return on the Friday following date of issue of the ticket by the 12.5 night train from Blackpool (North); due Euston 5.0 a.m. (Saturday morning).

Passengers desiring a ticket with an availability of more than one day should ask for a "MONTHLY RETURN TICKET," the return half of which is available on any day by any train within one Calendar Month from date of outward journey.

Third Class Monthly Return Fare to Blackpool 39/11.

FOR NOTES AND CONDITIONS, ALSO RESERVED SEATS, SEE OTHER SIDE.

Obtain the "Holidays by LMS" Guide, and plan your Holidays now.
16,000/1056   Mercury Press, Northampton.

◀ The great days of Charlton and Blackpool are recalled by this football excursion leaflet issued by the LMS in 1938. This so-called day trip would have tested the dedication of the fans, for they had to leave Euston at 1.30am and did not get back to London until 5am the next morning.

▲ A crowded diesel multiple unit sets off for a day at Redcar races in the early 1960s, maintaining a tradition of racing specials set in the mid-Victorian era. The railways democratized racing by making it accessible to the masses and, by doing so, can be said to have prompted the development of the enclosure, in which to contain them.

British Railways
SOUTHERN REGION

EPSOM RACES

Tuesday, Wednesday & Thursday
April 21st, 22nd & 23rd

Tuesday, Wednesday, Thursday & Friday
June 2nd, 3rd, 4th & 5th
(DERBY DAY WEDNESDAY, JUNE 3rd)

Saturday & Bank Holiday Monday
August 1st & 3rd

Friday & Saturday
September 4th & 5th

Frequent Train Services
TO
TATTENHAM CORNER
(ON THE COURSE)
EPSOM DOWNS
OR
EPSOM

FOR DETAILS OF FARES FROM LONDON AND A SELECTION
OF SUBURBAN STATIONS — SEE OTHER SIDE

— 8 MAY 1964

(4/38)   Stock
                                                                    (748 FF)

SOUTHERN RAILWAY.
EMPTY HORSE BOX
CLEANSED & DISINFECTED

At_____

Date_____

To _____

Date_____

Vehicle No._____

◀ In March 1967, near the end of the steam age, a football special approaches Leeds. Fans lean out and lavatory paper streams from the windows. By the late 1980s trains were regularly vandalized, and football specials soon ceased to run.

▶ This 1964 leaflet underlines the popularity of Derby Day. It points out that Tattenham Corner station is right on the racecourse, which even today is heavily railway dependent.

RAIL CENTRE: WREXHAM

IN ANY PRE-1950S railway map the Wrexham area is marked by an unusually dense cluster of stations, at least 15 in close proximity. This reflects the complicated railway history of the Wrexham region. The town was a meeting point for many lines in which larger companies had an interest, and its early history is marked by serious conflicts between the GWR and the LNWR. Later the Great Central joined the battle too.

As a result Wrexham had three stations, General, Central and Exchange. Today, after many closures and much simplification, the picture is much more

DENBIGH

As this 1930s postcard suggests, Denbigh's principal attraction is the ruined castle, high above the Vale of Clwyd. Also of interest is a market cross and a town hall dating to the 16th century. Trains first reached Denbigh in 1858, via a branch south from the Chester & Holyhead main line along the north Wales coast. In 1869 the route westwards from Wrexham was completed, through the efforts of the Mold & Denbigh Junction Railway. It was closed in 1962.

straightforward but the town still has two stations. One of these, General, is a handsome GWR structure of 1912 with pretty ironwork. First on the scene, in the 1840s, was the Shrewsbury & Chester Railway, but many others followed, notably the Wrexham, Mold & Connah's Quay Railway, which took over 20 years to complete its line, and the Wrexham & Ellesmere. Notable also in the area were the number of mineral lines, where passengers were very much a secondary concern. These included the branch to the collieries and iron works at Brymbo.

BERWIG

Berwig was the last of a sequence of little halts on the mineral line that ran south from Brymbo to Minerva. Coal and iron were the inspiration for the railway's construction from the 1860s, and both the LNWR and the GWR had an interest in it. As this card indicates, passengers were a lesser concern.

OSWESTRY

Oswestry, a market town with agricultural roots and delightfully set among hills, has an old-fashioned atmosphere with its timber-framed and 18th-century buildings. The largest Victorian building is the old station, an Italianate structure built in 1860 by the Oswestry & Newtown Railway. This card shows Cross Street in the early 1960s: it is a busy scene with plenty of period vehicles and shoppers enjoying the sunshine.

ELLESMERE

This romantic view of a suburban street in Ellesmere was posted in 1905, at which time the houses must have been relatively new. So modern a view gave little impression of the much older town, famous for its setting among meres, or lakes, but it reflected Ellesmere's expansion since the arrival, first of the canal and then, in the 1860s, of the railway. First to the town was the line from Whitchurch to Oswestry. Thirty years later Ellesmere became a junction with the opening of the Wrexham & Ellesmere Railway, which was worked by the Cambrian company until 1923. The headquarters of the Cambrian Railway, the largest independent company in Wales, was in Oswestry, so its impact on this region was considerable.

Snow at Wrexham General in 1962

WREXHAM

BRIDGE STREET, CHESTER

CHESTER

This 1950s view of one of Chester's major streets shows examples of the features that characterize the city, notably its timber-framed buildings and its elevated shopping arcades. For the inhabitants of Wrexham and its surrounding villages, Chester was an important shopping and leisure centre, a short train ride away. As a major railway city, it was also the starting point for longer trips.

CHIRK, AQUEDUCT & VIADUCT

CHIRK

In 1801 a massive stone aqueduct was completed at Chirk, to the designs of Thomas Telford, to carry the Llangollen Canal high above the valley of the river Ceiriog. At the time this was one of the wonders of the Industrial Revolution. Forty-seven years later another similar but even larger structure appeared alongside it, a 16-arched viaduct carrying the trains on the newly completed Shrewsbury & Chester Railway. Together, the two became one of the sights of this part of Britain, featuring in many 19th-century paintings and engravings. That their appeal continued into the 20th century is indicated by this 1930s version of a view that was by then very familiar and almost as famous as Chirk's 14th-century castle.

FROM THE CAB

IN THE EARLY DAYS of railways the drivers and firemen of locomotives had a miserable existence, working hard and for long hours in an unforgiving environment. Exposed to the elements, at risk of being burnt by hot iron and steam, and having to withstand the erratic and violent motion of the train with nowhere to sit and little to hold on to, the men on the footplate certainly earned their wages. At the same time, they carried a great responsibility for the safety of the train and its passengers. Roofed cabs did not appear until the 1870s and seats were rare until the 1930s. Even on the last generation of British Railways steam locomotives, fully enclosed and weatherproof cabs were unknown. With the cab always at the

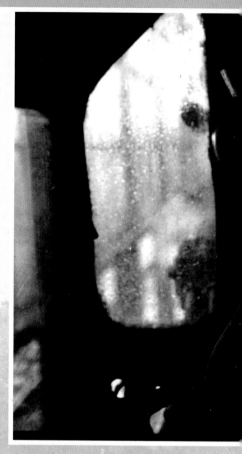

▲ Mainline steam ended in Britain in 1968 and enthusiasts rushed round the country to catch a last view of regular steam haulage. On a wet day in Manchester Victoria station, a Stanier Black 5 waits to depart, with the view from the cab caught for the last time. Sentiment apart, this shows how limited the driver's view to the front was, particularly in bad weather.

◀ In the latter part of its short life the Torrington to Halwill Junction line in Devon was little used. As a result, mixed passenger and freight trains were not uncommon. Here, in 1958, the driver looks back to check his train near Yarde. Two clay wagons, perhaps from the pits at Peter's Marland, sit between the coach and the guard's van.

▶ The Brighton & Dyke Railway, a short branch up onto the downs from Brighton, was opened in 1887. After a somewhat chequered existence, it closed in 1939. During the latter part of its life, the line was operated by Sentinel steam railcars, vehicles that offered drivers unusual comfort and a good view.

▼ When running in reverse, the driver often had to lean far out of the cab to have a reasonable view of the track ahead – no hardship on a sunny day, but unpleasant in the rain. This view was taken in 1959 near Frongoch, on the GWR Bala to Blaenau line.

rear of the boiler, forward vision was limited, so the driver spent much of his time leaning out of the side windows. When diesels and electric locomotives took over, things improved radically, with enclosed cabs at both ends and a central driving position.

The view from the cab has always had a particular appeal, mainly because, inevitably, it was the best view of the journey ahead, but also because it was a view that the passengers could rarely have. As a result, it was always a favourite for photographers and popular with film-makers. Nowadays that tradition has been maintained in modern, commercially made videos that show the view from the cab on journeys all over Britain, past and present.

MACHYNLLETH TO PWLLHELI

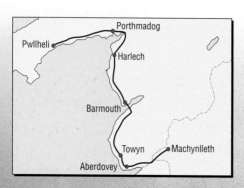

Mainline railways came comparatively late to north-west Wales, with promoters and investors perhaps discouraged by the difficult terrain, the lack of significant industry and the small population. In mid-Victorian Britain, tourism was still in its infancy and the pleasures of the Cambrian coast were still to be discovered. Things began to change in the 1860s, firstly with the opening in January 1863 of the Newtown & Machynlleth Railway, whose 22-mile line made the west coast of Wales accessible to Newtown, Welshpool, Oswestry and Shrewsbury. The route included the famous Talerddig cutting, for some time the deepest in the world. Meanwhile, further south, the Aberystwyth & Welsh Coast Railway had gained approval for a line northwards along the coast to Pwllheli, via Barmouth and Porthmadog. This was planned to connect with the Newtown line at Machynlleth. It was built in stages, with the section from Machynlleth

▼ On a hot day in the 1950s a locomotive simmers quietly at Dovey Junction, awaiting its next duty. The station is deserted, barrows are neatly parked and the signals are down – a common scenario at a station that came to life only when trains arrived.

south to Borth and Aberystwyth opening first. By the time it was finally completed in 1867 it, and most of its connecting lines, had been taken over by the Cambrian Railway. This company, after a shaky start, was well established by the 1880s, at which point tourist traffic was rapidly expanding. This kept it in business until it was absorbed into the GWR in the early 1920s.

The period from the 1920s to the 1950s represented the heyday of the line, thanks to the rapid expansion of the holiday trade. The beaches, landscape and history of west Wales were widely promoted, notably by the GWR itself, and a named train, the Cambrian Coast Express, began to serve the region. Hotels and

▼ Near Aberdovey the railway runs at the water's edge on an embankment overshadowed by great mountains. In this splendid setting a double-headed special makes its way along the shore, filled with passengers eagerly awaiting their day on the Talyllyn Railway.

holiday camps flourished. At the same time the line carried plenty of freight, including coal traffic from south Wales, thanks to its connections with lines to north Wales and to the Midlands and north of England via Shrewsbury and Chester.

From the 1960s the line declined rapidly as the freight traffic disappeared and the holidaymakers abandoned the Cambrian coast.

For a while, the section from Machynlleth north to Pwllheli was threatened with closure, particularly after the loss of nearly all the connecting lines, most notably the routes north to Caernarfon and Bangor and eastwards from Barmouth to Ruabon. In the south, the end of Aberystwyth's link to Carmarthen and Swansea made the Cambrian coast seem even more isolated. However, the line survived the Beeching era and in the 1980s was even improved by investment. This included the rebuilding of Barmouth bridge.

THE JOURNEY

Today the Cambrian Coast line offers a delightful journey, with a route that passes through a varied landscape, never far from the sea. There are glorious beaches and splendid castles to be seen, and connections with steam narrow-gauge railways.

The train for Pwllheli starts from Machynlleth where the gabled station, fully restored in the 1990s, offers passengers the pleasures of plenty of original detail. Adjacent is a small stone building, the station used by the narrow-gauge Corris Railway, a former slate tramway that carried passengers between 1880 and 1931. It was closed completely in 1948 after flooding damaged some of the trackbed. There is a museum in the old station and a short length of track has been relaid. After Machynlleth the Cambrian coast line follows the river Dovey to Dovey

BARMOUTH QUAY FROM ISLAND. A 298.

Junction, the connecting point for the line south to Aberystwyth. After the junction the line crosses the river and then runs right beside the sea to Aberdovey, a quiet and old-fashioned holiday resort and in the 19th century one of the busiest ports in Wales. At Towyn, whose church contains the earliest-known example of Welsh writing, there is a connection with the narrow-gauge Talyllyn Railway, a former slate line opened in 1866. Since 1951 it has been

▼ ▲ The appeal of Barmouth is timeless: its magnificent setting was as exciting to Victorian and Edwardian travellers, seeing the Welsh coastline for the first time, as it is now. This 1920s postcard underlines this. On the right is the railway, entering the town, after the dramatic crossing of the estuary on the longest wooden viaduct in Britain.

owned and operated as a tourist railway by a preservation society, the first line in the world to be saved in this manner. In the 19th century, Towyn harbour was filled with ships loading slate for destinations in Britain and around the world, but today little remains to hint at this once vital trade.

From here the train carves its way through rocky cuttings and then there is a fine view of Fairbourne's sandy beach and Barmouth Bay beyond. At Barmouth Junction, now Morfa Mawddach, the remains of the line eastwards to Bala, Llangollen and Ruabon can be seen. The section to Dolgellau, alongside the river Mawddach, is a footpath and cycleway.

The approach to Barmouth is magnificent, with the train slowly crossing the long viaduct over the Mawddach estuary. Completed in 1867, this, at 800 yards, is the longest wooden railway viaduct in Britain, and the last survivor on this scale of a type once common. Steel spans at the Barmouth end include one that used to open to allow ships to pass. The viaduct also carries a footpath.

After Barmouth the line runs slightly inland to Harlech, where the station sits far below the castle and town centre. Continuing on its inland route, the train passes through a series of small stations, Tygwyn, Talsarnau and Llandecwyn, with distant views across the estuary of the Dwyryd towards Portmeirion. Another wooden viaduct takes the train across the Dwyryd and then it curves round to Minffordd, where passengers can change for the narrow-gauge Ffestiniog Railway. This is the nearest station to Portmeirion, whose Italianate fantasy village is quite a walk away. The line then makes a long approach to Porthmadog across the marshland of the estuary, with a backdrop of distant mountains.

◀ Passengers on the train enjoying the unrolling panorama of the scenery can easily forget that the view of the train in the landscape is often as exciting. Notable is this view from the battlements of Harlech Castle, high above the little station and train, which are minor features in a huge coastline picture.

▲ While there are only glimpses of Portmeirion from the train, it is easy to visit Clough Williams-Ellis's fantasy Italianate village from its nearest station, Minffordd. This is also a connecting point for the narrow-gauge Ffestiniog Railway on its line inland to Blaenau Ffestiniog.

A busy town and formerly a major slate port, Pothmadog also offers visitors two narrow-gauge steam railways, the Ffestiniog up to Blaenau Ffestiniog and the Welsh Highland, whose old route towards Beddgelert and Caernarfon is being re-opened bit by bit. More significant is the work going on at the other end of this cross-country route. From the Caernarfon end, trains are already running again along over 12 miles of the former route, using remarkable articulated locomotives imported from South Africa.

After Porthmadog the line runs inland through woods and then returns to the seashore near Criccieth, whose castle is clearly visible from the train. Next is Afon Wen, the site of the former junction with the line north to Caernarfon and Bangor, and then Penychain, a station built to serve the Butlin's Holiday Camp. This is now a sad place, with long empty platforms redolent with the memory of holiday specials and the thousands of families who would have made their way from the train to the camp, laden with suitcases and buckets and spades, and bursting with excitement about the week ahead. The journey,

▶ Porthmadog harbour was greatly developed in the 19th century for the slate trade, and a century ago it would have been filled with ships loading finished roof slates for destinations in Britain and around the world. In this 1920s postcard some ships are at the quayside but the trade is already in decline. This view shows the magnificent setting that helped to give the region a new life as a tourist centre.

▼ By 1989 long locomotive-hauled trains were becoming a rarity on the Cambrian Coast line. With Penrhyndeudraeth in the background, a class 37 diesel hauls its train slowly across the curving wooden viaduct across the estuary of the Dwyryd, allowing its passengers time to savour the diversity of seaside landscape that makes this journey so exceptional.

Portmadoc Harbour.

and the line, ends at Pwllheli. Originally the terminus was outside the town, but in 1909 a new station was built nearer the town centre. This is a long, low gabled building in timber, stylishly elegant in an Edwardian way, and now a somewhat grand finale for the single track that remains.

The Cambrian Coast line, once the province of great expresses, holiday specials and freight trains, is now the epitome of the country railway. Little diesel railcars shuttle to and fro, serving limited local needs, and offering the visitor a memorable series of views and panoramas that combine landscape and history. This is the best seaside line in Wales, one of the best in Britain, and a classic rural railway journey.

▲ At Pwllheli holidaymakers could continue their exploration of the town and its seafront on a horse-drawn tram, a simple vehicle offering no protection against the weather. In typical interwar holiday style, everyone is well dressed and most are wearing hats, determinedly enjoying the breezy trip on the hard toast-rack seats.

SLATE

ALTHOUGH SOME had been in operation for centuries, the slate quarries of Britain were a Victorian phenomenon. Huge quantities of slate were produced: over 500,000 tons from Wales alone in 1898, the year of peak production. Not only did slate cover the buildings of Britain, it also was exported to many parts of the world. The quarries were generally inland, so railways were needed to transport the finished slates to the quayside. They came early, in railway terms, particularly in north Wales. The Penrhyn network started in 1801, Dinorwic in 1824 and Ffestiniog in 1836. These were narrow-gauge systems using gravity, rope haulage and horses to move the slate wagons. Steam came later, but the quarry railways remained self-contained, with idiosyncratic locomotives, rolling stock and operating practices, and with no link to the national network until the 1850s. Standard-gauge railways did not reach Blaenau Ffestiniog until 1879. Mainline railway connections encouraged the rapid expansion of the quarries, in Wales, Cornwall, the Lake District and Scotland, and by 1900 more slate was being transported by train than by ship. The industry declined steadily through the 20th century, with most of the major slate networks closing in the 1950s and 1960s.

▲ Slate quarry railways were quite distinct, with their own type of locomotive and a variety of specially designed wagons for transporting the finished product. Many of these remained in use for decades. Here, a line of loaded wagons travels along the main line in the Penrhyn system in 1961.

▼ Locomotives meet on the Dinorwic network in 1956, while a visiting enthusiast adjusts his camera. Dinorwic was a huge quarry and the first to use railways. The locomotive in the foreground has survived into preservation.

The Padarn Railway was opened in March 1843, to connect the Dinorwic quarries with the harbour at Port Dinorwic, and it finally closed in 1961. It was built to a 4ft gauge, one of a number used in the region. The network in the quarries at Dinorwic was 2ft. This photograph shows the locomotive 'Dinorwic' at work in 1956 near Lake Padarn. This locomotive has not survived, but part of the Padarn's route has been re-opened as the Llanberis Lake Railway.

► As late as the early 1960s the Penrhyn quarry was still busy, and large quantities of slate were being shipped from Port Penrhyn. In 1961 a typical locomotive hurries its train of loaded wagons towards the storage area on the quayside. At this point Port Penrhyn was served by both narrow-gauge and standard-gauge railways. Such scenes were soon to disappear for ever.

NARROW GAUGE

TODAY NARROW-GAUGE railways in Britain are associated entirely with tourism and preservation, with important and popular lines in Kent, Cumbria and, most significantly, Wales. Some are newly created, some are old lines re-born. Successful though they are, these lines in their modern form give little indication of the importance of narrow-gauge lines in the past. Throughout the 19th century and well into the 20th century Britain's railway map was hugely increased by a vast network of narrow-gauge lines, built primarily for industrial purposes. They served quarries, brickworks, military bases and depots, and a whole host of specialized industries from brewing to papermaking. Some were self-contained within the confines of a factory or quarry, while others had routes of many miles with mainline connections. Passenger carrying was often of secondary importance but, thanks to the cheapness with which they could be built and operated, narrow-gauge lines were increasingly used from the late 19th century to bring railway access to remote regions of Britain and to encourage the spread of tourism in areas such as Wales, north Devon and the Derbyshire Dales.

See the
Rheidol Valley

No visit to Aberystwyth is complete without an excursion to Devil's Bridge. British Railways' only narrow-gauge passenger trains enable you to enjoy twelve miles of the most magnificent scenery from Aberystwyth to Devil's Bridge.

The waterfalls, immortalised by Wordsworth, have to be seen to be believed.

DO NOT MISS THIS TRIP.

Day Return Fare 3/6

BY ANY TRAIN — ONE CLASS ONLY
4th June to 10th September 1960

Children under three years of age free; Three and under fourteen years of age half fare. Tickets valid outward and return on date of issue.

WESTERN REGION

PLEASE SEE OVERLEAF FOR DETAILS OF TRAIN SERVICES.

▶ Opened in 1902 from Aberystwyth to Devil's Bridge, the Vale of Rheidol was built for mineral and passenger traffic but from the 1920s was essentially a tourist railway. Always popular, it was long part of British Railways but is now independent. In 1973 'Llywelyn' takes water at Devil's Bridge.

▲ ▼ One of the Great Little Trains of Wales is the Welshpool & Llanfair Light Railway, opened in 1903 as a local line for freight and passengers. Below, in 1955, Lyons cakes are being loaded at Welshpool, where, as seen above, the rails used to run through the streets.

On the Manifold Valley Light Railway, Derbyshire, near Beeston Tor.   (North Staffordshire Railway)

▲ A famous example of a narrow-gauge line built largely for tourism was the Leek & Manifold Light Railway. Opened in 1903 and closed in 1934, it made accessible a hitherto remote region of Derbyshire. In 1937 the trackbed became a footpath and cycleway, a pioneer in this kind of re-use.

RUABON TO BARMOUTH AND BLAENAU FFESTINIOG

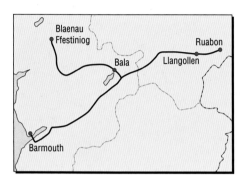

The railway from Ruabon to Barmouth was the creation of the GWR, ambitious to extend its empire to the west coast of Wales. It was built in short stages by nominally independent companies. The Vale of Llangollen Railway opened in 1862 and the Llangollen & Corwen's nine-mile line opened four years later. In 1868 the Corwen & Bala opened its short section, and the route was finally completed in 1870 by the Bala & Dolgelly Railway, which made an end-on connection with a short branch from Barmouth along the Mawddach estuary. To the south an equally tortuous scheme linked Welshpool with Machynlleth and the Cambrian Coast route, built by several companies that came together in 1864 to form Cambrian Railways, to the annoyance of the GWR. In time, the rivalry between the Cambrian and the GWR became intense, and at Dolgellau, where their routes met, they built separate stations. To some extent these two routes duplicated each other and both served a region that had neither a great population nor much in the way of industry and mineral resources. However, that was not the point. The main function of these lines was to give a degree of control in central west Wales to the GWR, whose primary aim was keeping the LNWR at bay. In the end, they all became part of the GWR.

▼ The most important structure on the Bala to Blaenau line is Cwm Prysor viaduct, seen here from an approaching train in 1959. Today this still stands, a monument to a little-used line that struggled through a tough and often spectacular landscape to no great benefit for its builders and investors in the 1870s.

B. 39398. LLANGOLLEN: FROM THE BRIDGE.

PRESERVED LINES

Preserved narrow-gauge railways are a famous feature of Wales, often marketed as The Great Little Trains of Wales. In fact, Welsh lines were pioneers in the national railway preservation movement, starting the whole thing at Talyllyn and Porthmadog in the 1950s. This route is unusual in that it has links with three preserved lines. First is the Ffestiniog, whose line from Porthmadog terminates at a new station built on the site of the old terminus of the GWR's branch from Bala. Second is the much more recent Bala Lake Railway, a narrow-gauge line built along the trackbed of the old Ruabon to Barmouth line as it runs beside Lake Bala. Third is the Llangollen Railway, the most important preserved standard-gauge line in Wales. Re-creating the spirit of the GWR in the 1920s and 1930s, it runs from Llangollen to Corwen, along the Dee valley.

▲ Posted in 1912, this card shows the river Dee and the adjacent station in Llangollen. By this time the tourist traffic was becoming significant and the station was often busy. Today, as the terminus of the Llangollen Railway, the station looks remarkably similar, although its style is the GWR of later years. Until the line was closed in the 1960s, trains continued off the bottom of the postcard to Ruabon, or away into the trees towards Barmouth.

▼ A landscape of gentle hills, woods and small fields accompanies the line on its route along the Dee valley west of Llangollen. In the 1960s, with closure on the horizon, a local train makes its way along the valley near Glyndyfrydwy, hauled by a GWR tank engine.

In time, the Ruabon to Barmouth line became a heavily used freight route, offering an alternative link from south Wales to the Midlands and the north via Carmarthen, Aberystwyth, Wrexham and Chester along GWR tracks. It was also kept busy with local cargoes, agricultural produce, livestock, timber and minerals.

The Beeching plan required only one route to the west coast of Wales and that was the Machynlleth line. All others were closed in the 1960s. Since then, parts of the Ruabon to Barmouth route have been re-opened as steam tourist lines. The Llangollen Railway operates standard-gauge services westwards towards Corwen, along the valley of the Dee, while further to the west the narrow-gauge Bala Lake Railway runs for a shorter distance along the southern shore of Lake Bala to Llanuwchllyn. As a result, little of the route is totally lost and exploration is easy, though more limited at the Ruabon end. At the other end, the section from Dolgellau to Barmouth is a cycle track, which is the perfect way to experience the delights of the Mawddach estuary. Most remote and harder to explore is the central section, from Corwen westwards to Bala, though the trackbed is often accessible from nearby roads.

▲ Seen here in the 1960s, Bala Lake Halt, also known as Bala Penybont, was a little-used station on the Barmouth line. Even the campers in the field have come by car. Today, this spot is alive again, as the Bala Lake Railway.

▼ Set against a dramatic sunset, a train bound for Ruabon crosses Barmouth viaduct in February 1965 on the first stage of its journey through the centre of Wales. The train has just left the three steel arches on the Barmouth end, the centre one of which could be swung to allow the passage of ships. The rest of the viaduct is wooden.

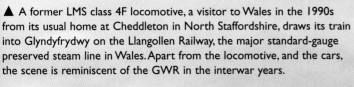

▲ A former LMS class 4F locomotive, a visitor to Wales in the 1990s from its usual home at Cheddleton in North Staffordshire, draws its train into Glyndyfrdwy on the Llangollen Railway, the major standard-gauge preserved steam line in Wales. Apart from the locomotive, and the cars, the scene is reminiscent of the GWR in the interwar years.

BALA TO BLAENAU FFESTINIOG

The GWR's ambitions were not limited to west Wales and the coast, for they also had their eyes on the north Wales slate traffic, and Blaenau Ffestiniog in particular. Unfortunately, the LNWR had similar ideas and began to plan an attack from the north, via an extension of the existing Conwy valley line. The GWR responded by backing the Bala & Festiniog Railway, whose 22-mile route from the south across difficult and hilly terrain was given approval in 1873. The race was on but, as both lines proved laborious and expensive to construct, it went rather slowly. In the event, the LNWR won, and its trains reached Blaenau in 1881. The GWR finally limped past the finishing post two years later. Both were able to benefit from the slate trade, but the legacy of their competition was that Blaenau Ffestiniog had two mainline stations, a couple of hundred yards apart but with no railway connection. This bizarre situation remained until 1960, when the GWR route south to Bala was closed in connection with the building of a nuclear power station at Llyn Trawsfynydd. As this was to be serviced via the Conwy valley line, a connection

▼ The most dramatic section of the line is around Cwm Prysor, where the trackbed can still be traced as it follows the contours and curves of the hillside. In this misty view taken in the 1990s from the trackbed in the foreground, the line of the old railway can be seen curving to the right above the steep fields. It is then carved into the rocky hillside in the distance.

◄ Photographed at the time of closure, Bala station already has an abandoned air. This is the town station, at the beginning of the branch to Blaenau. The junction station, though fully equipped, was rarely used by Bala passengers, and a shuttle train ran between the two for those using mainline trains at the junction.

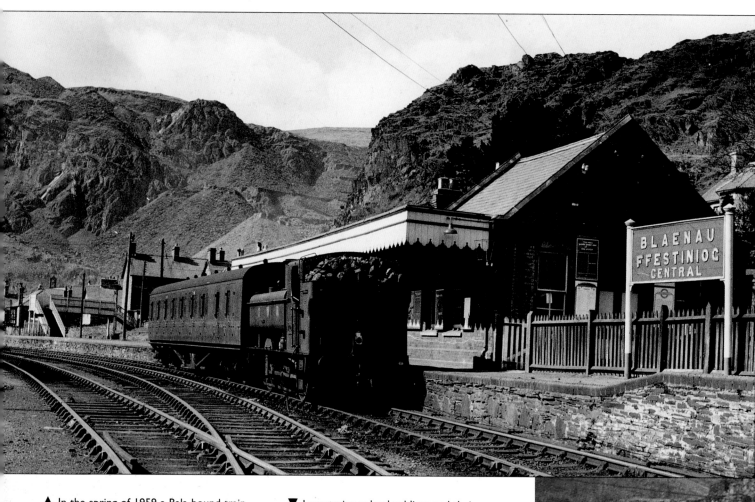

▲ In the spring of 1959 a Bala-bound train waits to depart from the former GWR terminus station, proudly called Blaenau Ffestiniog Central. The single carriage and the deserted air suggests that passengers were already rare. The other Blaenau station, for the Conwy valley line, is in the distance, overshadowed by the towering slate hills that determine the town's character.

▼ Long trains unload soldiers and their equipment at Trawsfynydd before World War I, perhaps Territorials at their annual camp in the area. Both tracks are being used, and one train includes a group of horse boxes. At this point the station is still being built; the platforms are unsurfaced, the lavatories await their roof, and the lamp standards their lamps.

had to be made in 1961. Later, Blaenau gained a new terminus station, built on the site of the old GWR one, and now used jointly by Conwy valley trains and the Ffestiniog Railway's narrow-gauge line from Porthmadog.

Exploration of the old GWR line to Blaenau is exciting as plenty survives in the wild landscape. There is not much to be seen in Bala itself but north of the town the route is clear. At Frongoch the station survives as a private house, then the trackbed climbs into wilder country before vanishing into the waters of Llyn Celyn reservoir, whose construction closed the line in 1960. The best section is around Cwm Prysor, with the trackbed alternating between embankments and cuttings. Often set on a ledge cut into the sweeping contours of the rocky hillside, it is seen easily from minor roads far below. It must have been a spectacular line, with echoes of railways in the Alps or South America. Surviving bridges and embankments, hint at something far more ancient and intriguing than a minor Victorian branch line. The line drops down the Prysor valley to Trawsfynydd, to a landscape of softer hills, woods and farms. The railway was kept open to this point, to serve the power station during its lifetime, so the route onwards to Blaenau is easy to follow.

▼ With the driver keeping an eye on the road ahead, the train from Bala approaches Blaenau in 1959, along a stretch of track set on a curving embankment to the south of the town. The character of Blaenau is apparent, surrounded by slate hills, and with terraces of houses roofed in the characteristic colour of the local slate. Until recently, this part of the route was still used for power-station traffic.

PUBLICITY

I N THE EARLY DAYS railways promoted their services through simple timetables, handbills and local advertisements, but from the late 19th century promotion and publicity steadily became more sophisticated. Decorative posters, postcards and brochures, emphasizing the pleasures and practicalities of rail travel, appeared for display at stations and travel agents and for distribution to the public. The heyday of publicity came after the Grouping of 1923, when the Big Four railway companies used modern advertising techniques to sell their services. Posters by leading artists, holiday guides and promotional booklets helped to make the GWR, the SR, the LMS and the LNER familiar all over Britain and abroad. Maps, lineside and route guides, walks books, jigsaws, histories and every kind of train book poured from the presses, all designed to encourage travel

NEWQUAY
ON THE CORNISH COAST **GWR**

▲ In the 1920s and 1930s paintings by contemporary artists, many specially commissioned, were issued as posters and gave the railways a new look.

and underline the modern image of the company that was issuing them. The GWR, the leader in the field, even published guides for anglers.

This comprehensive and modern approach to publicity was maintained by British Railways, and throughout the existence of the nationalized railway network colourful posters and brochures continued to encourage train travel all over Britain. Since privatization, the unified brand and carefully controlled image of the railways has been lost, although stylish publicity material is still being issued.

"Britain's Mightiest"

KING GEORGE V

A LIST OF THE TRAVEL PUBLICATIONS
OF THE GREAT WESTERN RAILWAY
WHICH FORM
THE LITERATURE OF
LOCOMOTION.

◄ The GWR was well known for its guidebooks, maps, postcards, jigsaws and other promotional publications. This catalogue of travel literature was issued in the 1920s.

► Stylish modern design was a feature of British Railways' publicity material. Typical is this 1970s map booklet for passenger use.

– travel by train

BRITISH RAILWAYS

NEWTOWN

BRITISH RAILWAYS

Passenger facilities and Map

1848

WATERLOO STATION CENTENARY

1948

HELEN McKIE

PRICE **1/6**

BRITISH RAILWAYS

FULLY ILLUSTRATED

British Railways

Passenger travel & map folder

▲ The tradition of using artists to promote travel was maintained by British Railways, as in this 1960s booklet.

▲ Conscious of its history and keen to promote a modern image, British Railways issued many special brochures, such as this, for Waterloo's centenary.

▼ Many companies issued official postcards during the Edwardian era. The LNWR claimed to have sold 11 million by 1914.

LANGDALE PIKES, AMBLESIDE
L. & N.W. RAILWAY.

Northern England

CARNFORTH TO CARLISLE VIA BARROW

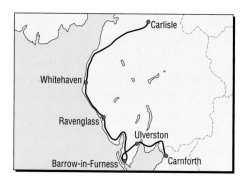

▼ On 2 August 1968, just days before the ending of steam on the British Railways network, a Standard class 4MT locomotive runs tender-first alongside Morecambe Bay with a few trucks for Ulverston. This scene, familiar from 150 years of railway history, was about to disappear for ever.

In any competition for the best country railway in Britain, the Cumbrian Coast line would have to be a strong candidate for the prize. It offers travellers a special blend of landscape and history as it explores in a notably leisurely way one of England's most remote regions. However, the best thing about the journey is the sea, and the quality of light created by its almost constant proximity. No railway in Britain offers so many miles of unbroken seaside, and for large parts of the journey the train is virtually on the beach. In winter the waves fling themselves towards the track and their spray covers the train.

Today not many people travel on this route and its survival seems perennially precarious, but it was not always thus. The Cumbrian Coast line was an early railway, its route open by 1850. Several companies were involved in its creation but they all shared a common inspiration, the desire to exploit the mineral wealth of the region, notably the deposits of coal and iron ore. It all started in 1837 when the Maryport & Carlisle Railway, with the advice of George Stephenson, began to build its line westwards from Carlisle. Things went slowly and the line was not completed until 1845. By this time a southern extension was being built by the Whitehaven Junction Railway, another Stephenson enterprise. This opened two years later. The third component was the Whitehaven & Furness Junction, which added a further 33 miles south from Whitehaven to meet, as its title implied, the ever-expanding network of the major player in the region, the Furness Railway.

◀ Grange-over-Sands was a railway resort, built to exploit the soft landscape and sandy beaches of Morecambe Bay. Although it was the Furness Railway that was instrumental in the town's creation, this promotional postcard was published by its much bigger rival, the LNWR – a reflection of the battle for tourist traffic in the Edwardian era.

▶ The legacy of the Furness Railway lives on in many parts of the Cumbrian Coast line. Outstanding is Ulverston station – grand, decorative and, when the branch to Lakeside on Windermere, was open, a suitable gateway to the Lakes. There are also plenty of small-scale structures, such as signal boxes. This one, visited in 1994, is at Foxfield, near Broughton.

▲ The Furness Railway believed that Seascale had great potential as a holiday resort and began to develop what had been a little village. A new timber-framed station was built and hotels were encouraged but, sadly, the idea never caught on and no one came. Today Seascale is still just a remote place beside the sea, with echoes of what might have been.

Ambitious and independent, the Furness quickly absorbed its local rivals and spread its handsome red locomotives over a network that eventually included more than 400 miles of railway. The power behind the Furness was the discovery in 1850 of enormous haematite deposits near Barrow, the exploitation of which brought great wealth to the railway and the region as a whole. Barrow, Whitehaven, Workington and Maryport all became flourishing harbours, and a large network of predominantly industrial lines spread inland to serve the mines and the many local iron and steel works. When there was a slump in the iron business in the 1880s, the Furness turned its attention towards tourism. Branches to Coniston and Windermere gave it a commanding position in the Lake District, while to the south, in Morecambe Bay, it was involved in the development of resorts at Kents Bank and Grange-over-Sands. However, the heart of its network, and its wealth, was always Barrow, particularly after the arrival of Vickers, the ship-building and munitions giant.

WASTWATER AND GREAT GABLE.   SEASCALE STATION.

◀ From the late Victorian era the Furness Railway relied increasingly on tourist traffic and did much to encourage it. This old postcard, published by the railway, shows Wastwater and Great Gable. These were not on the Furness network but were accessible from Seascale, which the company was hoping to turn into a resort.

▼ Amid lengthening shadows a diesel railcar crosses the estuary of the Esk south of Ravenglass, on one of the long viaducts that characterize the line as it crosses a sequence of river estuaries between Ravenglass and Carnforth.

▼ Near Foxfield, the Lakeland hills make an exciting backdrop to the railway as it runs along the shore. This is a journey of amazing landscape quality, and the windows of a modern railcar make a great viewing platform.

The Furness remained independent until 1923, when it became part of LMS. By then the writing was on the wall, and from that point its network was steadily pruned. By the 1960s all that remained was the original line along the Cumbrian coast and there seemed no logical reason why that should survive. It served dying industries and decaying old towns, there was a much quicker route from Lancaster to Carlisle along the West Coast main line, and wonderful landscape has never kept a railway open. Its unlikely saviour was the Windscale nuclear plant, now Sellafield, at Seascale, and to this day the trains continue to run.

THE JOURNEY

The Cumbrian Coast line starts at Carnforth, where it leaves the West Coast main line, entering immediately a more attractive landscape as it reaches the Kent estuary, which it crosses on a long, low viaduct. It is now by the sea for the first

▲ This busy scene at Whitehaven station in 1968 shows that there was plenty of traffic then, with long locomotive-hauled trains still using the route.

time, flanking Morecambe Bay and passing the old resorts of Grange-over-Sands and Kents Bank. Another long viaduct takes it over the Leven estuary, and then the train is in Furness territory: Ulverston, Barrow, Broughton and Millom. The best bit of the journey soon begins, the long seaside route northwards though Ravenglass, where it meets the narrow-gauge Ravenglass & Eskdale line, to the failed resort of Seascale and the old red stone of St Bees. Next comes the former industrial belt of Whitehaven, Workington and Maryport, an exciting stretch marked by glorious scenery, picturesque remains of industry and towns built in the 18th and 19th centuries.

At Maryport the train turns inland, to run through hills and farmland to Carlisle, via Aspatria and Wigton. Carlisle Citadel station, with its rich, Tudor-style stone façade, is the fitting ending for a journey that encompasses some of the best scenery in England and the history of the last two centuries.

Citadel Station, Carlisle

◀ This 1905 postcard shows the neo-Tudor extravagance of Carlisle Citadel station, designed for the Lancaster & Carlisle and Caledonian railways by Sir William Tite and completed in 1850. It is still a fine climax to a glorious journey.

▼ British Railways did its best to encourage traffic in this region with promotional tickets, as this 1963 handbill indicates. Within a couple of years closures had made the circular tour impossible.

▼ A northbound single Sprinter hugs the coast as it passes Sellafield on the single-track section between Braystones and Nethertown.

PLEASE RETAIN THIS BILL FOR REFERENCE

TRAVEL
—ALL DAY
—ANY DAY
WITH
WEST CUMBERLAND AREA
DAY-LINE TICKETS
ISSUED ANY DAY
28th APRIL TO 26th OCTOBER, 1963

WEST CUMBERLAND AREA DAY-LINE TICKETS ARE AVAILABLE BETWEEN CARLISLE, WHITEHAVEN, PENRITH AND INTERMEDIATE STATIONS SHOWN IN THIS MAP.

SECOND 10/- CLASS CHILDREN 3 & UNDER 14 5/-

FIRST CLASS, ADULTS 15/-; CHILDREN, 7/6

DOGS, CYCLES OR PRAMS ACCOMPANYING PASSENGERS, 5/-

Day-Line Tickets are available for day of issue only for unlimited travel by any train (steam or diesel) between any stations within the area. Break of journey is allowed at any intermediate point.

TICKETS CAN BE OBTAINED IN ADVANCE AT STATIONS AND OFFICIAL RAILWAY AGENTS.

Further information will be supplied on application to the Stations, Official Railway Agents, or to Mr. R. R. BUTTER, District Manager, Citadel Station, Carlisle, Telephone 25411, (Extn. 6), or to Mr. E. I. BOYD, District Manager, Barrow-in-Furness, Telephone 1445.

March, 1963. *Travel in Rail Comfort* BR 35000

LONDON MIDLAND

Barrow Printing Co. Ltd., Lawson Street, Barrow. Q A I.

TRAIN CREW

UNTIL THE LATTER part of the 20th century a typical train crew comprised driver, fireman and guard, a tradition unchanged since the early days of the railways. Initially a brakesman, the guard gradually became more important as his duties expanded to include control of the train and its safety, care of the guard's van and everything travelling in it, the checking and, later, the issuing of tickets. The guard was also an important figure in the eye of the public, and had a uniform to underline this. The driver and fireman were, by comparison, largely invisible yet their responsibilities and skills were enormous, and they had to work closely together. Traditionally, drivers started as cleaners at the locomotive sheds, looking after the engines, progressed to become firemen and then ultimately drivers, a process that took some years. As firemen and drivers they worked first on goods trains, before progressing to passenger trains. Train crews worked as a team to carry out their complex duties and were mutually dependent. They were also proud men who enjoyed their skills and their status, despite the pressures of the job. Accordingly they did not mind being photographed, either informally, or posed with their locomotive.

▲ One of the many duties of the footplate crew was the collection and care of the token which controlled single-line working. This once universal process has now been rendered obsolete by radio and electronic control methods. Here, in 1959 at Trawsfynydd on the Bala to Blaenau branch, the driver exchanges tokens with the signalman.

◄ Footplate men of the Victorian era were proud and powerful and their locomotives were often immaculate, despite the primitive, dangerous and dirty conditions in which they worked. They seem to have posed willingly for photographers. In this image from the 1880s, the driver, fireman and, unusually, the guard stand on the footplate of their North Eastern Railway locomotive.

▲ As the London to Edinburgh express waits at Doncaster during the long, hot summer of 1976, there is time for the guard to relax, have a smoke and pass the time of day with a maintenance engineer armed with a wheel tapper's hammer.

◀ The narrow-gauge slate railways of North Wales made particular demands on train crews and working conditions were generally more primitive than elsewhere. Clearly, however, these men were just as willing to pose for the camera with their well-worn but nonetheless well-cared-for locomotive.

TRACK REPAIRS

FROM THE EARLY DAYS of the railways, maintenance of the track and the railway infrastructure was undertaken manually by gangs of platelayers or 'gangers', sometimes also known as waymen or – as in modern parlance – permanent way men or trackmen. A gang, under the control of a foreman and with a lookout armed with a hooter and flags, would be responsible for a length of track, usually a couple of miles, to be inspected twice a day, and maintained as required. Using a range of hand tools, they were responsible for the alignment, gauge and level of the track, for replacing sleepers, rails or chairs as necessary, for adjusting ballast, for checking points and for maintaining drains, culverts and lineside fences. Tools and equipment were kept in platelayers' huts placed regularly along the track, and often equipped with a stove. The derelict remains of these can still be seen all over the network. Trolleys were used for

the transport of tools and materials. Major engineering works involved larger gangs and the closure of the line, usually at weekends. In 1948 over 60,000 permanent way men were employed by British Railways.

From the 1960s, mechanization, prefabricated welded track and new technology changed completely the world of track maintenance. By the 1990s there were 12,000 track maintenance staff, and now the work is done by outside contractors.

◀ The weed-killing train is part of the regular pattern of track maintenance. In August 1993 a weed-killing train passes the old Maentwrog Road station on the Trawsfynydd branch in north Wales, now itself closed.

▶ A permanent way gang poses for the camera in 1950, taking a break from laying a new stretch of track. At this date, this was an arduous and largely manual task.

▲ Weed control was part of the platelayers' regular workload until weed-killing trains were introduced in the 1930s. Here, Southern Railways uses retired locomotive tenders to distribute the liquid.

▲ In 1956 two gangers pause from their track-maintenance work on a stretch of the Welshpool & Llanfair narrow-gauge railway, then a public railway but now a famous preserved line.

SETTLE TO CARLISLE

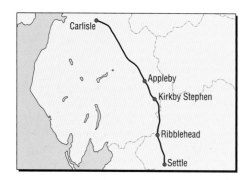

In an era of intense competition and extreme ambition, the Midland Railway, based in Derby, stood out from other companies. It was determined to become a railway of national importance and to this end it had constructed at St Pancras one of London's largest and most expensive termini. The same spirit drove its directors to build a new route to Scotland, to challenge the monopoly of traffic that was held by the LNWR and the GNR. J S Crossley, the Midland's chief engineer wanted a route through the heart of England, and one that would avoid those steep gradients that for most trains demanded extra locomotives.

The route Crossley chose, from Settle Junction near Leeds, on the existing Midland network, to Carlisle, ran for 73 miles through some of England's most inhospitable and underpopulated landscapes. It certainly crossed the heart of the country, and by dint of superb engineering Crossley managed to create a line that climbed to 1,169 feet and then dropped nearly to sea level without any serious gradients. To achieve this, he needed 13 tunnels, 21 viaducts and the expenditure of a vast sum of money, which the Midland had no real hope of recovering. Building the line required an army of up to 7,000 labourers, many of whom had to work through the extreme conditions of Pennine winters, armed only with picks

▼ Landscape is the defining quality of the Settle to Carlisle route, and panoramic views can be enjoyed from the train window. Much of the route crosses high moorland; here the wild bareness of Blea Moor is softened by summer sunshine as a class 2 diesel hauls a southbound mixed freight along the line in 1967.

◄ This old card shows Settle's position in the local landscape. The railway line's elevated route through the town can be seen in the centre of the postcard.

▼ The classically bleak landscape around Blea Moor has been broken up by conifer plantations. Taken in the spring of 1984, this photograph shows the north end of the tunnel, the longest on the line, as a Carlisle-bound express emerges headed by a Peak class locomotive. At this time the debate about the line's future was beginning, with closure being the likely outcome.

▲ Smoke and steam, sunshine falling on the moorland landscape, and a bridge that blends perfectly with the scenery – elements that express the special quality of the Settle & Carlisle. On a good spring day in 1966 a Stanier class 5 locomotive hauls a mixed freight up Aisgill.

▼ Having escaped the threat of closure in the 1980s, the Settle & Carlisle has been enjoying a new lease of life. Stations have been re-opened and restored in the old Midland Railway style. Typical is Garsdale, seen here on a sunny day in 2003, with no one in sight and not a train to be seen, but wholly characteristic of the Settle & Carlisle.

and shovels and living in windswept shacks. It was the last main line in Britain to be built by hand. Severe weather delayed its building, and has plagued its operation since.

When opened in 1876, the Settle & Carlisle fulfilled its owners' ambitions, enabling the Midland to run its trains directly from London to Scotland. Its route was slower than those of its rivals but it was well connected, via the Midland's large and ever-expanding network, so there was plenty of traffic. Freight quickly became important, establishing a pattern of use that was to make the line invaluable in both World Wars. As part of a through route, the Settle & Carlisle was vital. As an independent line, it made no sense, serving only three small towns, Settle, Kirkby Stephen and Appleby, with a combined population of about 7,000. This, along with its high maintenance costs, meant it was threatened with closure on several occasions, most recently in the mid-1980s, when it was saved by a nationwide campaign backed by local authority support. It is a remarkable survivor today, a living memorial to Victorian ambition and endeavour, and to the skills of the engineers and labourers who built it.

▲ A southbound mixed freight headed by an LMS Stanier class 5 crosses Artengill viaduct in 1967, a classic Settle & Carlisle image. Both the type of freight train and the steam locomotive were soon to be consigned to history.

THE JOURNEY

The journey offered by the Settle & Carlisle is one of the best landscape experiences on Britain's railway network. From Settle, a handsome stone town spread out below the railway, the line climbs steadily into the wild and barren landscape of the Yorkshire Dales, initially following the valley of the Ribble. The 24 stone arches of the great Ribblehead viaduct, the route's most famous feature, can be seen from the train as it approaches it. Next in the series of excitements is Blea Moor tunnel, carved by hand for well over a mile, 500 feet beneath the moorland. This, and

◄ Always a busy place, Carlisle Citadel station was host to seven different English and Scottish railway companies in the late Victorian and Edwardian era. By the 1920s it was under the control of the LMS. Built originally in 1847, the station was enlarged several times. The vast airy iron-and-glass roof apparent in this 1920s photograph, was added after the arrival of the Midland's Settle & Carlisle line.

Ribblehead, took five years to build. Another viaduct, Dent Head, leads to Dent station, the highest in England and a remote spot favoured by walkers. After crossing the summit at Aisgill, the train starts the long descent to Carlisle, through the valley of the Eden. Spectacular vistas are interspersed with viaducts and tunnels. The scenery softens as the train approaches Kirkby Stephen, which until the 1960s was a meeting point for two great trans-Pennine railways. The descent from the fells continues to Appleby, another fine old market town, still dominated by its castle. From here, the line is never far from the Eden, by now a broad river flowing through a wooded valley. The landscape opens out on the approach to Carlisle and takes on a more gentle aspect, a quiet climax to a glorious journey. The Settle & Carlisle is a remarkable experience because of its route and because of the stylistic continuity of the structures, both stations and engineering features, rarely so unaltered on so long a line.

▼ Extreme winter conditions in the Pennines gave the railway's builders a miserable time and have often disrupted services. However, snow is part of the Settle & Carlisle experience, enjoyed here near Birkett by lucky passengers on a special hauled by two classic preserved locomotives, a Midland compound and the Jubilee 'Leander'.

IRON AND STEEL

F ROM THE 1840s, for over a century, the destinies of three major industries, railways, iron and steel and coal were closely linked, with each developing to serve the needs of the others. Railways were users and prime movers of coal, much of which was moved round the country to fuel the iron works. Railways were also responsible for the movement of iron ores at first from the mines in many parts of Britain and later, when imported ores began to replace local supplies, from the docks. Railways made possible the movement of raw materials over long distances, for example the shipment of ores from Cumbria to steel works in Cleveland, and the return shipment of coke from Durham to Cumbria. Railways also transported the products of iron and steel works – ingots, rolled sections, bars, castings and forgings. Until the 1960s all this was moved by the railways, but the latter part of the 20th century witnessed a steady reduction in the production in Britain of coal, iron and steel and a corresponding reduction in rail traffic. Of course, the railways themselves have always been major users of iron and steel, with many railways owning foundries. Typically, a mile of track requires over 200 tons of iron and steel.

▲ Wagon labels from the 19th century reveal the interaction between the railway, the coal industry and the iron and steel industry. They also show what huge quantities of raw materials and finished products were moved around the country.

▶ In October 1989 a long train of flat wagons loaded with locally made rolled steel sections moves slowly out of Tees yard, hauled by two matched diesel locomotives.

◀ The Edwardian lady cyclist looks rather out of place against the backdrop of the massive Balkan Vaughan iron works in Cleveland, a major producer at that time.

▲ Many iron and steel works had their own railway systems, with miles of sidings and foundry lines to handle the specialized traffic, as shown in this 1960 photograph.

▲ In 1967 a rare steam age survivor hauls a load of steel tubes through the Lune Gorge, on the West Coast main line.

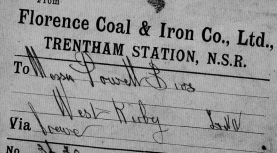

From

Florence Coal & Iron Co., Ltd.,
TRENTHAM STATION, N.S.R.

To *Messn Powell Bros*

Via *West Kirby LNW*

No ......3630...... Date ....1.12.03....

RAIL CENTRE: HULL

PLACED AS IT IS on the remote north bank of the Humber estuary, Hull has always had to look after itself. In railway terms, this meant setting up a company, the Hull & Selby, to ensure that the line from Leeds was extended as far as Hull. This was completed in 1840 and the port began to flourish as a result. Other lines were added, to York via Market Weighton, to Scarborough via Beverley and Driffield, along with branches to Hornsea and Withernsea. Most were built independently, but soon they all became part of the North Eastern's ever-expanding network. Another route opened from the south, via New Holland Pier and a ferry service across the Humber. The only attempt to break the NER's monopoly was the setting up in 1880 of the Hull & Barnsley Railway. Its rival route eastwards along the Humber and its own dock complex opened in 1885 but was never a great success. Finally swallowed by the NER in 1922, it has subsequently all but disappeared. Hull was a thriving

YORK

Many major stations were accompanied by railway hotels and York was no exception. This massive pile, the Royal Station Hotel, was built by the Northern Eastern Railway in 1878, a clear statement of the company's power, wealth and influence at the time. Seen here in 1908, it looks much the same today, although it is no longer a railway hotel. The important line from Hull to York was built by the ubiquitous York & North Midland Railway.

centre, with at least eight stations using the Hull name in their title, along with goods and dock depots. Today, only G T Andrews' great Paragon station survives in use, but Hull Trains maintain the spirit of independence.

8552   SELBY ABBEY

SELBY

For centuries a centre of industry and an inland port, Selby is dominated by its massive abbey, as this 1950s view indicates. Founded in the 11th century and much enlarged over subsequent centuries, the abbey is famous for its early stained glass. Beyond is the river Ouse, the source of the town's prosperity. The Leeds & Selby Railway reached the town in 1834 and built a rather small and inconvenient terminus station. When the Hull & Selby arrived in 1840, it built a new through station, so the old one was closed to passengers, one of the first such closures in Britain. It remained in use for freight until the 1970s.

BEVERLEY

A wealthy medieval cloth town, Beverley has great churches, wide streets and splendid buildings of many periods. Its spacious elegance is typified in this Edwardian view of the market place, which – as in so many views from that period – is remarkably empty. The ambitious York & North Midland opened its station here in 1846, and it still has a generous iron and glass train shed over the platforms, though it is not G T Andrews' original twin-span version. From Beverley trains ran westwards towards York and northwards to Driffield and then onwards to the Yorkshire coastal resorts of Bridlington, Filey and Scarborough. Rather surprisingly, the latter is still open, keeping Beverley, and its station, on the railway map.

MARKET PLACE, BEVERLEY.

Hull Paragon station in 1981

HULL

HORNSEA

Although this card was posted in 1916, the message indicates that it was written on holiday. It shows various views of Hornsea's beach, promenade and seashore, along with the Mere, Yorkshire's largest freshwater lake. Popular in the 19th century as a resort, Hornsea acquired its own branch line in 1864 but lost it a century later. Along the line was Goxhill, one of Britain's last market-day-only stations, which continued to open once a week until 1953.

Sprotboro' Lock, near Doncaster

DONCASTER

Sprotborough Lock is a picturesque place south of Doncaster on the Sheffield & South Yorkshire Navigation, a waterway route to Sheffield along the river Don. Posted in 1918, the card shows a loaded barge waiting to enter the lock, in a setting that is still recognizable. Canals and river navigations dominated trade in the north-east until the coming of the railways, and some waterways remained busy until the latter part of the 20th century, mostly for the carriage of coal. From an early date Doncaster was a major centre of railway activity, with many routes passing through the town. It was also the site of one the Britain's largest railway works. Trains from Hull could go via Goole or Selby.

SMOKE AND STEAM

NOW THAT STEAM locomotives are seen only on preserved railways and the occasional mainline special, they tend to have an aura of romance and nostalgia, and the smell of the smoke and the steam is a vital part of the experience. Human memory being notoriously fickle, it is easy to forget the reality of life in Britain when so much depended on coal and steam, the byproducts of which were smoke, ash, dust and grime. A steam locomotive was a complex and often unpredictable machine requiring constant attention, regular maintenance and skilful firing and driving if it was to work efficiently and cleanly. Sometimes maintenance was skimped, the machinery was worn out, the coal was not of good quality and the footplate crew were careless. Then the results could be poor performance and mighty emissions of smoke and steam, effects that now are often seen as the true spectacle, power and magic of the steam age.

▼ Two classic LMS mainline passenger locomotives, 'Princess Beatrice' and 'Duchess of Norfolk', demonstrate the power of steam to a group of young train enthusiasts on a wet day in Carlisle station in 1960.

▶ In June 1962 a Paddington-bound express roars through Box station, in Wiltshire, hauled by a GWR Castle class locomotive that is laying down a thick smokescreen.

▲ The most modern and efficient British locomotives were the large class 9Fs of the late 1950s, some of which had mechanical stoking. Nevertheless this one, in charge of a mixed freight, is colouring the blue sky black.

▲ A GWR tank engine blasts off clouds of steam at Paddington, to the consternation of a smartly dressed passenger.

▶ On a cold and wet January morning in 1966 a British Railways Standard class locomotive makes an explosive start from Cole station on the Somerset & Dorset line.

COCKERMOUTH TO DARLINGTON

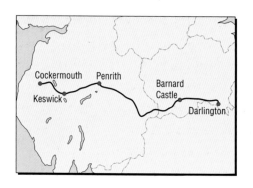

▼ In 1968 a diesel railcar crosses a girder bridge east of Keswick, on the last surviving section of the route, from Keswick to Penrith. This finally closed in 1972, despite pressure to keep it open as an access route to the Lakes.

In the north of England, geography determined that the major railways tended to run north–south, and few lines were built specifically east–west. Those that did faced the challenge of the Pennines and a landscape that demanded heavy, expensive engineering. Nevertheless, such routes were required for cross-country freight traffic, and particularly for the movement of coal, coke, iron ore and haematite.

One such route was the South Durham & Lancashire Union Railway, whose line from a junction near Bishop Auckland across the Pennines to Tebay on the Lancaster & Carlisle's main line north opened in 1861. It linked Kirkby Stephen and Barnard Castle via a high Pennine summit at Stainmore. Immediately successful, it remained a busy freight route until its closure in 1965. It also encouraged the building of other lines, for example the Eden Valley Railway north from Kirkby Stephen to Appleby and thence to a junction with the Lancaster & Carlisle just south of Penrith. This line, completed in 1862, also connected with the Midland's grand Settle & Carlisle north–south route at Appleby, but for all that it was a relatively minor undertaking with only a single track. The next link, westwards from Penrith, opened in 1865 under the auspices of the Cockermouth, Keswick & Penrith Railway. This was a scenic 31-mile route across the Lakes via Troutbeck, Greta Gorge and Bassenthwaite. Its construction upset the Wordsworth family, fervent opponents of all railways in the Lake District. In the event, no railway did more to open up the region to tourism and the line was doubled in 1900. At Cockermouth there was a connection with the line to Workington, opened in 1847, and thence to Carlisle, Barrow and Lancaster.

S 4285   RAILWAY STATION, COCKERMOUTH.

▲ In this early 20th-century photograph passengers crowd the station platform at Cockermouth, underlining the popularity of the line as an access route to the Lake District before the coming of the motor car. No trace of the station remains today.

The final link in this complicated chain of railways already existed. Opened in 1856, this was the Darlington & Barnard Castle Railway, a nominally independent operation but actually part of the Stockton & Darlington's expanding empire. The Stockton & Darlington had at its famous opening in 1825 launched the railway age, and by the 1850s was a rich and powerful company that had made Darlington the heart of a busy network. Its name was destined for ever to be synonymous with railway history.

The result of all this was a railway across the north of England that linked the west and east coast main lines to Scotland. It was an important freight route, and its scenic splendour gave it great tourist potential. As such, it continued to be busy until the days of British Railways, having retained its importance as a connection between the LMS and the LNER. However, from the 1950s freight diminished and traffic fragmented into a series of local journeys, often handled by diesel railcars. Closures began in 1962 with the Penrith to Kirkby Stephen section. Within a few years much of the route had disappeared, leaving only a local service from Penrith to Keswick which, despite its value as environmentally friendly access to the Lake District, finally disappeared in 1972. One short section, from Kirkby Stephen to Warcop and accessed via the Settle & Carlisle line, was kept open for military traffic until the 1990s.

THE ROUTE TODAY

Exploring the route of the railway today is a mixed blessing. Some sections are inaccessible and some have disappeared, while others have acquired a new life as official footpaths, cycle tracks and bridleways. However, the track of the railway is

▼ The line is closed and trains no longer call at Bassenthwaite Lake. Flowers decorate the track and everything awaits demolition. Nothing remains today to identify the scene.

Hitherto remote and inaccessible, the Lake District became popular early in the 19th century, coincidental with the development of the English railway network. Despite strong objections from leading literary figures such as William Wordsworth and John Ruskin, railways began to creep into the region. First came the Kendal & Windermere's branch line from Oxenholme, opened in 1847. Twelve years later the branch line to Coniston was completed. Both lines encouraged the development of connected steamer services, which marked the beginnings of modern Lakeland tourism. However, the only railway that ever crossed the Lake District from west to east was the Cockermouth, Keswick & Penrith, completed in 1865. By then, objections were more muted and popular Lakeland tourism was getting into its stride, thanks particularly to this railway.

▼ On a cross-country route memorable for its scenery, the trackbed sweeps clearly through the landscape east of Threlkeld, overshadowed by Saddleback and Lonsdale Fell. Despite its great quality and appeal, much of the trackbed is still on private land and therefore inaccessible.

still easily found on the map, even if it is not always so visible on the ground. It is a memorable route to follow, partly because of the quality of landscape through which it passes and partly because, in relative terms, there is still plenty to see. Starting at the Cockermouth end is initially unrewarding, thanks to the obliteration of much of the route by the A66, but Braithwaite station survives as a private house. A better starting point is Keswick, where the station stands forlorn but almost complete and from here there is a proper path along the track to Threlkeld, a lovely walk along the route of the river Greta with iron girder bridges still in place. East of Threlkeld the line is often visible, but inaccessible, through glorious scenery, a pattern maintained to Penrith, where trains still race along the West Coast main line. After Penrith the trackbed comes and goes, but a surprising number of station buildings survive as private houses, a feature of the line as a whole. The most exciting section is from Kirkby Stephen to Barnard Castle, the line climbing through a wild landscape to the great summit level on the moors of Stainmore. Always in view as a permanent mark on the landscape but generally inaccessible, the trackbed hints at the difficulties inherent in building and running such a line. Wind and weather fought against the trains, mostly heavy freights, often double-headed or with banking engines at the rear, and in winter it could be closed for days by snow. It is a bleak but memorable environment. There were many viaducts, none more famous than the American-style, high iron trestle at Belah, of which no trace remains. Stations survive, at Barras and Lartington, echoes of the activity brought to this remote region by the railway.

Barnard Castle is a handsome town but there is no trace of its once-busy station where four lines met. There is more to be seen to the east, with stations surviving at Broomielaw, Winston, Gainford and Piercebridge, as well as other railway structures. Broomielaw, which survives in an abandoned state, appears to have served no more

▼ In the summer of 1961 a passenger train crosses Stainmore Summit, 1,370 feet above sea level, on its way eastwards to Barnard Castle and Darlington. Today the trackbed through this wild landscape is clearly visible from the road on the right.

Cockermouth, Keswick and Penrith Railway.

Date, 27 . 5 . 191 5

From **THRELKELD**

To Longtown N B

Via Pen Carlisle

Consignee, Murray

Owner and No. of Waggon, 248

Owner and No. of Sheets } and Under Sheets, }

than a couple of buildings at the end of a very minor road; in fact it was once very busy, thanks to a long-gone army camp nearby.

A useful aid to the explorer is the survival of a surprising number of cast-iron plaques attached to buildings and bearing the letters S&DR, memorials to the builders of this part of the route. A more substantial memorial is the stone bridge that carried the track over the river Tees near Gainford, one of the few major engineering features still to be seen. Further east is the site of the junction with the branch south to Forcett, a quarry line opened in 1866. This is a remote and magic spot that stirs thoughts of erstwhile railway life.

The route originally ended at Hopetown Junction on the line north towards Bishop Auckland. Remarkably, this remains in use, so Darlington's famous North Road station, a classical structure dating from 1842 and a key monument to Britain's early railway history, still has real trains, as well as a railway museum.

▶ An Edwardian view of Barnard Castle, from a series of similar scenes published as postcards by the Great Northern Railway to encourage tourism. Dating from the 12th century, the castle was largely destroyed by Cromwell's troops during the Civil War. Far less visible today is Barnard Castle's railway history, with nothing to be seen of the station where four lines used to meet.

▼ The most astonishing structure on the route was the great iron trestle viaduct at Belah, a type of bridge more commonly associated with America than Britain. Here, in the 1960s, shortly before the closure of the line, a passenger train crosses high above the steep river valley, double-headed as so often to cope with the weather and the gradients. After closure the viaduct was demolished, leaving only the abutments as a record of spectacular engineering.

STONE

IN THE 18TH CENTURY quarries were pioneer users of primitive, horse-drawn railways, so it is no surprise that they were among the first to use trains in the early decades of the railway age. Local quarry lines soon opened in many parts of Britain, and by the 1850s many railway companies were realizing the potential that lay in moving stone in bulk over long distances. As a result local stones such as Bath, Portland and Scottish granite began to be used in building projects far afield. Later, with a rapid increase in demand for crushed stone for road building, railways again made the most of the opportunity by developing limestone quarries in Derbyshire, Durham, Yorkshire, Somerset and elsewhere. A number of lines, for example Buxton to Ashbourne, were built primarily for stone traffic, and many quarries were railway-owned. Today, a number of quarries, not least Merehead in Somerset, still give the railways plenty of business.

Railways themselves have always been major users of stone, both for the initial building of the network and continuously, for trackbed ballast, which is usually crushed limestone or granite, often from dedicated quarries such as Doveholes in Derbyshire or Meldon on Dartmoor.

▲ Quarries frequently have their own railway system, for loading and marshalling the hoppers. In the past this was a well-known habitat of the industrial steam locomotive. Some survived in use long after the end of steam on the main lines, but today it is all diesel, as seen here at British Gypsum's Mountfield quarry.

▼ Still in service in 1965, an old LMS Stanier class 5 hauls a loaded track-maintenance ballast train past Shap quarry sidings, high on the West Coast main line. The train has two guard's vans, so it can be moved in either direction while distributing the crushed stone ballast.

▲ As this photograph makes clear, the Derbyshire dales have been scarred by centuries of quarrying on a massive scale, and never more so than in the years since the coming of the railways. In the dramatic landscape of Miller's Dale, on a summer's day in 1989, a line of hoppers filled with crushed limestone is hauled slowly from the quarry by a pair of class 37 diesels in contrasting liveries.

▼ The carriage of crushed stone has always required a range of specially designed wagons, or hoppers, made in huge quantities by both railway wagon builders and independent engineering firms such as Dorman, Long. Typical is this 1920s example, looking immaculate in a publicity photograph. Wagons used for railway ballast were often equipped with distribution shutes and other means of spreading the crushed stone on the trackbed.

HULL TO SCARBOROUGH

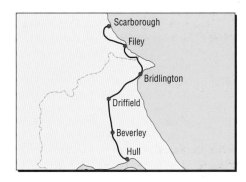

Hull was an early railway town, with lines from Leeds and Selby in use by 1840. Others soon followed, opening up the landscape of east Yorkshire. Within a few years most of these had been absorbed by the York & North Midland Railway, and it was this company that oversaw the building of a line north to Scarborough via Beverley, Driffield, Bridlington, Filey and Seamer. This was in operation by 1846.

Many of the line's stations were designed by G T Andrews, a leading railway architect of the period, and a number survive relatively intact – enough to give a flavour of early 19th-century railway building styles and to make the line a memorial to his skills. Grand and ambitious stations at Hull and Scarborough contrast with his cottage-style country stations along the line at Lockington, Hutton Cranswick, Nafferton and Burton Agnes. At Beverley, Bridlington and Filey he constructed stations with delicate iron train sheds. Of these, Filey remains relatively unchanged.

In the 1840s most of the railways in this region were under the control of the infamous speculator, George Hudson. After his fall in 1848 the companies survived independently but in 1854 many, including the York & North Midland, were brought together to form the North Eastern Railway. With a network of 720 miles, this was the largest railway in Britain at the time. It survived various ups and downs but continued to expand and operate successfully until the Grouping in 1923, when it became a part of the LNER. Much of it lived on into the British Railways era, but in the 1960s the network north

▼ Well named, Hull's Paragon station was a large and spectacular building from the day of its opening in 1846. The architect was G T Andrews, a key figure in railway history in the north-east. Later extensions did not significantly alter its quality, as is apparent in this Edwardian postcard view. Today, inevitably, this sense of spacious elegance has been lost.

PARAGON STATION AND SQUARE - HULL.

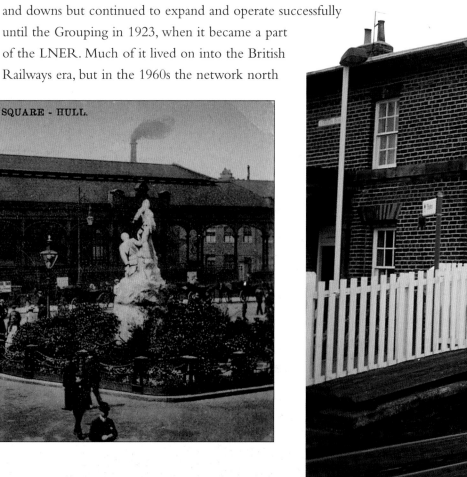

◀ Nearing the end of its life, an old D20 class locomotive waits at Driffield at the head of a special in June 1957. Young trainspotters are making the moist of this rarity. Within a few months this veteran had been scrapped. Driffield station has also changed since this photograph was taken: it has lost its canopies and as a result looks rather bare.

▼ Amid a plethora of modern signage, Nafferton retains a strong flavour of the early 19th century. The cottage-style station is intact, though now a private house. With the main building set at right angles to the platform, and a bow window marking the former waiting room, it is an example of G T Andrews' distinctive style.

of Hull was considerably reduced. Among the losses were the lines to York via Market Weighton and Pocklington, Malton, Hornsea and Withernsea. The Scarborough route was a rare survivor, thanks in part to its long association with the holiday resorts it served. By comparison, the Scarborough to Whitby line, another famous holiday railway, with a more spectacular route, was lost. Today the railway map of east Yorkshire is very empty, with the Hull to Scarborough line very much on its own.

THE JOURNEY

In its heyday, this line was regularly visited by long expresses, many of which were specials serving the holiday camps along the coast. Today, only short diesel railcars shuffle to and fro, serving primarily the needs of local commuters, school children and shoppers.

From Hull the line goes due north across an open landscape of farmland broken by low hills and patches of woodland. Stations at Beverley and Driffield hint at past glories but there are plenty of details, architectural and railway, to

▲ 'Donkeys on the Beach at Bridlington', the title of an old postcard that captures the traditional atmosphere of this famous east coast seaside resort.

▼ Bridlington was a resort made by the railway. In the 1950s most holidaymakers travelled by train. For these families, watching the arrival of the empty special that will take them back to York, the holiday is over.

catch the eye. At Lockington and Hutton Cranswick, G T Andrews' country-style station houses can be enjoyed, simple brick buildings set sideways to the track, with distinctive hipped roofs and grand classical porticos. From Driffield the line turns towards the coast, with Bridlington Bay coming into view before the station. This is still a substantial and well-detailed building, even though the iron roof has gone. Rounding Flamborough Head, the train now takes an inland route parallel to the coast to Filey. The station here, though smaller, is largely original and still has the iron train shed designed by Andrews. Recently restored, it is now one of

the best of its type still in regular use. After leaving Filey, the line turns westwards, to run inland to Seamer, where it joins the line from York to Scarborough for the short run into the town's magnificent terminus, again by Andrews. Expanding traffic caused the station to be extended regularly, but without affecting its character. One of these extensions included the building of what is still claimed to be the longest platform bench in the world. The build-up of excursion traffic from the Edwardian era required the construction of a separate excursion station, and as late as 1934 the main station was still being enlarged. In the 1960s it all went into reverse and large parts of the station were taken out of use. The effect of this, combined with careful restoration, has been a return to the station of the 1840s.

Today, Scarborough's grand station, and grand hotels, are reminders of the town's glorious past as the best resort on the north Yorkshire coast. It is still a popular place, with plenty to offer visitors, but the great days of the station are long gone. Diesel railcars creep in from York or Hull, pale and insignificant ghosts of the vast holiday expresses and long-distance trains for which it was built.

▲ This Edwardian card shows the grandeur of Scarborough station and its clock tower, one of the greatest creations of G T Andrews. It looks much the same today.

▼ In the summer of 2003 a diesel unit in a garish colour scheme enters Scarborough. The sidings are overgrown and empty but the semaphore signals hint at more glorious days.

EXCURSIONS

THE FIRST EXCURSION trains were run at the dawn of the railway age, and in 1844 it was said that the railway excursion was 'our chief national amusement'. The big event that put the excursion on the map was the Great Exhibition in 1851, when millions travelled to London by train. Since then railway companies have generally viewed the excursion as an easy way to make money, using spare vehicles at off-peak times. Victorian excursions were often on a huge scale. One carried 1,710 people in 46 carriages from Brighton to London. Others covered vast distances, with passengers sleeping on the train. Bank Holidays, sporting occasions, club and social outings, tourism, shopping trips, exhibitions and shows, works outings – all were grist to the excursion mill, and many were widely promoted. Under British Railways, excursions became less common, due largely to a shortage of vehicles, and today they are almost extinct.

▲ The Lancaster & Carlisle Railway completed its 69-mile route in 1846. By 1851, the year of the Great Exhibition, it was in effect part of the LNWR and was thus able to advertise day excursions to London for the exhibition. Similar excursions were operated that year by virtually every railway company in Britain, bringing millions to London for the first time.

▼ In this evocative Edwardian photograph, the members of a Welsh temperance group outing pose at Llangollen station before departure. It is a proud moment: many families are present and the locomotive bears a special headboard. Today, no doubt, Health and Safety would take a dim view of all those people standing on the track.

▲ This Southern Railway booklet of 1928 shows that excursions to the coast were so regular they were almost in the timetable.

◀ Excursions taking railway enthusiasts on unusual journeys to remote parts of the network and little-used stations have always been popular. This predominantly male activity has occasionally involved families, as this 1950s photograph of a tour on the old Stafford to Uttoxeter line shows. The station is Chartley & Stowe, and everyone is probably watching the locomotive running round its train.

▶ Excursion marketing was often adventurous. This 1958 example offers 'a fascinating combination of events': an outing to Pitlochry to see the play *The Ghost Train*, hauled by a famous preserved steam locomotive.

(1421) **G.W.R.**

EXCURSION

To

▼ In 1961 an exceptionally long diesel multiple unit pauses at Woodburn en route from Blyth to Billingham, near Middlesbrough, for an agricultural show – a typical excursion special.

BRITISH RAILWAYS

B 24889

"THE GHOST TRAIN"
at Pitlochry Festival Theatre
Saturday, 6th September 1958

RAIL EXCURSION
TO
PITLOCHRY

by "The Festival Special"
Engine 123 and the two ex-Caledonian Railway Coaches

ON SATURDAY 6th SEPTEMBER
Including

★ A BOOKED SEAT AT THE AFTERNOON PERFORMANCE OF "THE GHOST TRAIN" AT PITLOCHRY FESTIVAL THEATRE.

★ LUNCH AND HIGH TEA AT THE GREEN PARK HOTEL OR AT THE FESTIVAL THEATRE RESTAURANT.

ALL-IN COST
(RAIL—LUNCH—THEATRE SEAT—HIGH TEA)

38/-

(Children 3 years and under 14 years—29/6)

OUTWARD			RETURN		
GLASGOW (Buchanan Street)	... lve.	a.m. 9 25	PITLOCHRY	... lve.	p.m. 7 15
PITLOCHRY	... arr.	p.m. 12 15	GLASGOW (Buchanan Street)	... arr.	9 50

Accommodation on the train is limited and passengers are requested to book well in advance for this very attractive outing. Tickets can be obtained at Buchanan Street Station or at British Railways Town Office, 37 West George Street, Glasgow.

HERE IS SOMETHING NOVEL—
A FASCINATING COMBINATION OF EVENTS!

A rail journey by the famous "old timer" Engine No. 123 ; a visit to the Festival Theatre to revel in the mysterious happenings of the celebrated comedy thriller of the century—
"THE GHOST TRAIN."

All information regarding Excursions and Cheap Fares will be supplied on application at Stations or to E. Lees, District Passenger Manager, 50 George Square, Glasgow. Telephone DOUglas 7080.

NOTICE AS TO CONDITIONS.—Tickets are issued subject to the British Transport Commission's published Regulations and Conditions applicable to British Railways exhibited at their Stations or obtainable free of charge at station ticket offices.

B.R. 35000—AE—July, 1958

H. Paton & Sons Ltd., Edinburgh

Scotland

DUMFRIES TO STRANRAER

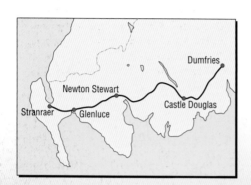

As railways spread their tentacles across the face of Britain in the 1840s and 1850s, competition between rival companies became increasingly intense. A notable reason for this was the desire to dominate the trade routes to Ireland. This prompted a number of railways to develop harbours and ferry ports on the British coastline between Wales and southern Scotland. One such was Portpatrick, a little fishing village on the far west coast of Wigtownshire. In 1850 the Glasgow & South Western Railway, an ambitious company, had completed its line from Carlisle to Glasgow via Dumfries. With one eye on the Irish trade and the other on its rival the Caledonian Railway, the G&SW decided to build a line westwards from Dumfries to Portpatrick via Castle Douglas and Stranraer. Actually built by the Portpatrick Railway, an associate of the G&SW, this was completed in 1862.

▶ After leaving Castle Douglas the line followed the eastern shore of Loch Ken, along a route that can easily be discerned from a minor road on the opposite shore. It must have been a delightful journey in the evening light. The loch is crossed by this three-arch, bow-string viaduct, which, remarkably, still stands.

◀ ▼ A major rail centre with routes in five directions, Dumfries was always popular with tourists. It was a thriving community with plenty of history, as this postcard implies. From time to time, it was also the setting for events such as the Royal Highland Show. This British Railways leaflet of 1954 promotes travel to the show from very distant places, indicating its extraordinary popularity at that time. Most of these routes have vanished.

BURNS WALK.

SWEETHEART ABBEY

HIGH STREET

DUMFRIES

CAERLAVEROCK CASTLE

OLD & NEW BRIDGES.

T. 2052

BRITISH RAILWAYS

Royal Highland Show
EXCURSIONS
TO
DUMFRIES
FOR THE SHOW
WEDNESDAY 23rd JUNE

OUTWARD		Third Class Return Fares.	RETURN	
	a.m.	s. d.		p.m.
Morpeth ....dep.	6 20		Dumfries ....dep.	6 15
Acklington .... "	6 35		Coldstream ....arr.	9 20
Alnmouth .... "	6 50		Norham .... "	9 35
Chathill............ "	7 5	**20/0**	Berwick .... "	10 0
Belford .... "	7 20		Belford .... "	10 20
†Berwick .... "	7 28		Chathill............ "	10 35
Norham .... "	7 55		Alnmouth .... "	10 55
Coldstream .... "	8 15		Acklington .... "	11 5
Dumfries ....arr.	11 40		Morpeth .... "	11 25

†—Change at Tweedmouth in each direction.

LIMITED DINING ACCOMMODATION WILL BE AVAILABLE ON THIS TRAIN.

Children under three years of age, free ; three years & under 14 years, half-fares.

TICKETS CAN BE OBTAINED IN ADVANCE FROM THE STATIONS AND ACCREDITED RAIL TICKET AGENCIES

Further information will be supplied on application to the stations, agencies, or to S. Cott District Passenger Superintendent, British Railways—Newcastle, Tel. 20741.

CONDITIONS OF ISSUE

These tickets are subject to the conditions of issue of ordinary passenger tickets where applicable and also to the special conditions as set out in the Bye Laws and Regulations and Conditions in the Public Notices

Luggage Allowances set out in the General Notices

Published by British Railways (N.E. Region)–6/54   Printed in Great Britain   T.P.W. Ltd. N/cle-B124

Regular ferry services to Ireland never
operated from Portpatrick, despite the
hopes and ambitions of the railway's
builders. The first scheduled service
started from Stranraer in 1872 with the
Princess Louise, a vessel custom-built for
the route. From then Stranraer never
looked back, and by 1907 ferries were
carrying motor vehicles as well as
passengers. In the late 1930s the first
stern-loading vehicle ferry came into
use. The route was much expanded, first
for military use and then to cater for
burgeoning tourism. Another new ship,
Princess Victoria, custom-built in Glasgow,
was introduced in 1947. Six years later,
on 31 January 1953, she was lost with
all hands in a violent storm that forced
open the stern doors. This was the
worst ferry disaster in British history
until the capsizing of the *Herald of Free
Enterprise* in Zeebrugge in 1987.

However, with promised government and admiralty support unforthcoming, Portpatrick was never developed as a ferry port, and regular ferry services to Larne, in Ireland, did not start until the early 1870s. By that time the emphasis had switched to Stranraer, a much bigger and better harbour, and in 1875 the railway began to carry mail over this route. Branches were opened to Kirkcudbright and Whithorn, and a more direct route to Stranraer from Glasgow via Girvan greatly increased the use of the harbour and its ferry services. Through-sleepers from London were introduced, tourism steadily increased, and from 1907 the ferries also carried motor vehicles. At this point the line was operated by a committee set up by the main rivals, the Glasgow & South Western, the Caledonian, the LNWR and the Midland, all keen to maintain their share of the Irish trade. During both world wars the route was heavily used by the military, and in the early 1940s a new harbour was built at Cairnryan with its own rail connection from Stranraer. Designed to be used if Glasgow or Liverpool were closed by bombing, it did not in the event come into its own as a ferry port until the 1960s, by which time the railways were on their way out.

Despite the rapid postwar development of Stranraer harbour, the decision was made to abandon all the railways west of Dumfries and to service Stranraer via the Glasgow and Girvan route.

▼ In 1963, in a view that gives some sense of the bleak and windswept setting, a mixed freight crawls over the Big Water of Fleet viaduct. At this time the viaduct did not have a guard rail and the train as a result looks very exposed.

Bit by bit the network was closed, the branches to Portpatrick and Whithorn first and the remainder by June 1965.

THE ROUTE

When it was built, the line crossed an isolated and relatively uninhabited area of bare hills, wild moorland and open farmland, quickly becoming the backbone of development in the region. Extensive forestation in the 20th century radically altered the landscape, so it is not always easy to find traces of the route today. Large sections are completely invisible and inaccessible but sometimes the line of the trackbed across the landscape can be identified. The stations that survive highlight the remoteness of the route, which seems at times consciously to avoid the towns and villages that could have benefited from its presence. The nature of the landscape caused many problems for the line's builders and made its construction expensive. Much of the money was swallowed by the major bridges along the route, notably those across the Black Water of Dee and Loch Ken, and the 20 massive stone arches of the Big Water of Fleet viaduct, still a splendid and dramatic sight as it strides across the inhospitable landscape. Elsewhere, two stone arches from the Craddoch viaduct survive, preserved and manicured without any context and as a result looking like some medieval relic. Also notable is the tall and elegant Glenluce viaduct.

The last section of the route, along river valleys and across

▲ Set as it was in the middle of nowhere, six miles from the small town it was designed to serve, Gatehouse of Fleet station must have seen very few passengers, even during the railway's busy years. Traces of the station remain, including this overgrown platform, a reminder of a once-important railway line.

▼ The most impressive monument to the line is the viaduct over the Big Water of Fleet. Curving slightly at one end, it has 20 arches 70 feet high. The lumpy brick encasing of the piers spoils its elegance when seen at close quarters but from a distance it makes a wonderful sight, striding across the bleak moorland. Like most of the viaducts on the route, it was completed in 1861.

213

▲ In the summer of 1963 the down freight has paused at Creetown, east of Newton Stewart. The locomotive has detached a single wagon and is about to shunt it into a siding while the rest of the train waits on the main line. Creetown station was an unusual building by Sir James Cowans.

softer farmland towards the coast, is more gentle and appealing. At Challon Junction, in sight of the sea and sandy beaches, the old line ends where it met the alternative route to Stranraer via Girvan, which is still busy with traffic. Stranraer Town station is long gone, and all trains now end their journey at Stranraer Harbour, a gloomy place overshadowed by the ghostly remains of a better past. Ferries come busily to and fro but few people now bother to use the train. The old route from Stranraer to Portpatrick, the reason why the line was built in the first place, is still to be found, climbing and cutting its way through the hills, and then dropping steeply to the site of the original terminus, expensively carved from the rocky cliffs high above the village, and with very limited facilities. An even steeper branch served the little harbour, an altogether impractical arrangement that makes it hard today to believe that anyone in the 1860s could really have seen Portpatrick as a vital element in the battle for the Irish trade. The harbour branch closed in the 1870s, when it became clear that the future lay in Stranraer.

▲ From an old bridge near Kirkcowan, midway between Newton Stewart and Glenlucen and in scenery typical of the line, the muddy track that was once this busy and essential railway stretches away silently into the distance.

◄ In the early 1970s Stranraer harbour was busy with trains and ferries, and proper boat trains were still running. Today it is a gloomy place and the trains are almost irrelevant.

► This postcard of Stranraer shows clearly the extensive harbour developments that started once it was established as a major ferry port for Northern Ireland. Military use in World War I prompted further expansion.

20478

Stranraer. General View.

TUNNELS

THE TECHNIQUES of tunnelling developed by canal engineers in the 18th century – that is, excavation by hand from shafts sunk from the surface – were unchanged by the first generation of railway builders. Work was slow, arduous and dangerous, and made unpredictable by the uncertainties of local geology. Some early tunnels, such as Box tunnel on Brunel's GWR near Bath, took years to complete. Later, steam power and improved explosives speeded the work, and from the 1870s the tunnelling shield, invented for the first Thames tunnel, was increasingly used. By the early 1830s there were tunnels over a mile long in use, the first trans-Pennine route was opened in 1840, and by 1870 there were 28 tunnels in Britain more than a mile in length. A further twenty-three were built in the next 35 years, the longest, at 4½ miles, being that under the Severn. Many had grandiose or ornamental portals, reflecting the achievement and pride of their builders. Today more than a thousand railway tunnels are still in regular use.

WORKING SHAFT, KILSBY TUNNEL, JULY 8TH 1837

▲ Inevitably the most famous and the longest tunnels steal the thunder, but all over Britain there are hundreds of lesser examples, many of which posed similar challenges for both engineers and builders. Typical is the short Seaton tunnel, in the north-east of England, which boasts a handsome castle-style portal. This is seen here in 1961 as a diesel-hauled mixed freight rumbles towards it at a cautious speed.

▲ Issued by the LNWR in 1905, this card commemorates the building of Kilsby tunnel, near Rugby, started in 1835. Kilsby proved to be one of the greatest challenges facing Stephenson as engineer of the London & Birmingham Railway. Construction of the massive work took years and was a continuous battle against quicksands and flooding.

◄ A dark, forbidding entrance portal in decorative brick frames Kemp Town tunnel, near Brighton. Some time in the Edwardian era the signalman looks out for an approaching train. Note the bell on the signal box.

► A famously decorative tunnel portal is Clayton, on the London, Brighton & South Coast Railway's line to the south coast. With battlements and turrets, this reflects the fashionable gothic style of the 1840s. The impact is rather weakened by the tunnel-keeper's cottage perched on top.

CLAYTON TUNNEL. L.B & S.C.R.

GLASGOW TO OBAN

The railway to Oban was born out of the fierce competition between those two rival Scottish companies, the North British and the Caledonian. The battle was about opening up the west coast of the Highlands for tourism, freight and specialized local traffic such as fish. First on the scene was the Caledonian, through its backing of a small, independent railway, the Callander & Oban. Set up in 1865, this company was perennially short of money, so its line westwards from Callander was built in fits and starts. Services were finally opened to Oban in July 1880. Quickly successful, the railway did much to develop Oban as a modern resort. It also played a major role in promoting the popularity of Mull and the other islands accessible by steamers from Oban. For a few years the Callander & Oban, and thus the Caledonian, operated unchallenged, but the North British soon had its eye on this new source of traffic and in 1889 backed the setting up of the West Highland Railway. Opened throughout to Fort William in 1894, this expensive and heavily engineered line through a wild landscape linked Glasgow directly to the western Highlands for the first time. The two lines met at Crianlarich, but each company built its own station, and maintained a sense of independence. Later developments in the region by the North British and the Caledonian included the long

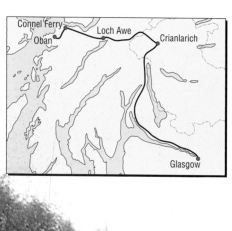

▼ Big, locomotive-hauled trains were a feature of the Oban route until relatively recently, giving a sense of grandeur completely lost in the modern age of the diesel railcar. In 1961 two paired diesels haul a scheduled service along Glen Lochy.

branch to Mallaig from Fort William, opened in 1901, and the Ballachulish branch north along Loch Linnhe from Connel Ferry, a few miles outside Oban. Things remained the same until the 1960s, under LMS and then British Railways' control.

The western Highlands did not escape the closures of the 1960s that devastated so much of Scotland's railway network. The Ballachulish branch closed in 1966, but the great steel-girder bridge across the entrance to Loch Etive survived, for use as a road. More significant was the obliteration of every line east of Crianlarich, severing the links to Dunblane and Perth. All that remained was the West Highland route from Glasgow to Fort William and Mallaig, and a fragment of the old Caledonian network in the form of a branch line from Crianlarich to Oban. A connection was made at Crianlarich to allow trains on the West Highland line to join the Oban branch, and the old Caledonian station, Crianlarich Lower, was abandoned. As a result, Oban services start from Glasgow.

THE JOURNEY

The West Highland line is a spectacular journey, a long single-track route from Craigendoran, on the Clyde near Dumbarton, to Fort William. The route is through Faslane and then along the shores of Loch Long to Arrochar, and thence

▲ In 1960, steam was still dominant on the Oban line. Here, on a bright day, a train drifts across the more open landscape east of Taynuilt, overshadowed by Ben Cruachan. The role played by the railway in opening up an inaccessible landscape cannot be overstated.

▼ Highland lines were almost invariably single track, to reduce construction costs of railways serving small populations in a challenging landscape. This modern view is typical, and timeless, giving a sense of the journey's visual excitement and colour.

northwards by Loch Lomond. From here the line climbs to Crianlarich. The best part of the route is the section north of Crianlarich, through Bridge of Orchy and high across Rannoch Moor, but the southern part is not to be scorned, with a long sequence of fine vistas in colours typical of the Highlands. Notable also are the stations, built to a standard pattern, which echoes a Swiss chalet, and set on an island platform to allow trains to pass on the otherwise single track. The station buildings are exceptionally pretty, sometimes with matching signal box. This sequence of stylistically matching stations on one line is unique in Britain.

From Crianlarich westwards to Oban the route is distinctly different, although initially it runs parallel to the Fort William line, branching away along Glen Lochy only after Tyndrum, another spot with separate stations built by the rival companies. Woods and hills lead to Dalmally, which for a while – when the Callander & Oban's money ran out yet again – was the line's terminus. The line then flanks the northern shore of Loch Awe, offering a good view of the ruins of Kilchurn Castle.

▼ Today, Connel Ferry bridge is a remarkable sight, clearly built as a railway bridge, even though it now carries road traffic. Always famously narrow, it is still single-tracked, with traffic-light control.

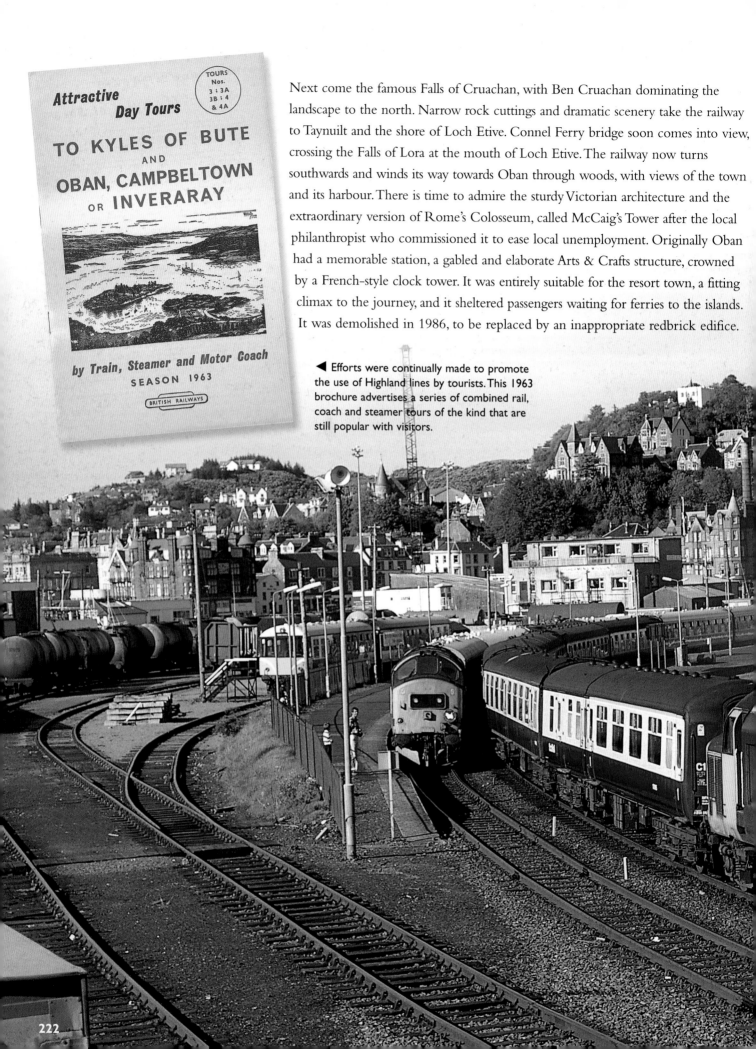

Next come the famous Falls of Cruachan, with Ben Cruachan dominating the landscape to the north. Narrow rock cuttings and dramatic scenery take the railway to Taynuilt and the shore of Loch Etive. Connel Ferry bridge soon comes into view, crossing the Falls of Lora at the mouth of Loch Etive. The railway now turns southwards and winds its way towards Oban through woods, with views of the town and its harbour. There is time to admire the sturdy Victorian architecture and the extraordinary version of Rome's Colosseum, called McCaig's Tower after the local philanthropist who commissioned it to ease local unemployment. Originally Oban had a memorable station, a gabled and elaborate Arts & Crafts structure, crowned by a French-style clock tower. It was entirely suitable for the resort town, a fitting climax to the journey, and it sheltered passengers waiting for ferries to the islands. It was demolished in 1986, to be replaced by an inappropriate redbrick edifice.

◀ Efforts were continually made to promote the use of Highland lines by tourists. This 1963 brochure advertises a series of combined rail, coach and steamer tours of the kind that are still popular with visitors.

Attractive Day Tours

TOURS Nos. 3 : 3A 3B : 4 & 4A

TO KYLES OF BUTE
AND
OBAN, CAMPBELTOWN
OR INVERARAY

by Train, Steamer and Motor Coach
SEASON 1963

BRITISH RAILWAYS